# Alive in Christ, Alert to Life

## C. JOHN WEBORG

COVENANT PRESS
CHICAGO, ILLINOIS

ISBN 0-910452-63-6
Copyright © 1985 by Covenant Press
Design: David R. Westerfield
Cover Photo: Neal Nicolay
Back Cover Photo: Olan Mills

**COVENANT PRESS**
3200 West Foster Avenue, Chicago, Illinois 60625
(800) 621-1290, (312) 478-4676

# CONTENTS

# PREFACE

Books, like rivers, have tributaries that feed them. This one is no exception. In 1978 I received an invitation to give the Adolph Olson Memorial Lectures at Bethel Theological Seminary, St. Paul, Minnesota, which were then presented in February, 1980. This became the core of the book which has now more than doubled in size. It is my pleasure to thank the seminary community for their hospitality to me. In particular I want to offer thanks to the then dean, Dr. Gordon Johnson, for the courtesies extended to me; to Dr. Donald Madvig, then professor in the Department of Biblical Literature and his wife, LaVerne, my hosts and good friends; to Dr. Richard Daniels, then dean of students, for attentiveness to the many details that made one's stay so enjoyable; and I am happy to acknowledge the work of the present dean, Dr. Millard Erickson, in bringing arrangements to completion. My regret is that the book took so long to be completed.

The expansion of the lectures into a larger work was occasioned by invitation from the Centennial Committee of The Evangelical Covenant Church to write a book on spirituality as a contribution to the Covenant's Centennial celebration (1885-1985). I am most grateful to the president of the Covenant, Milton B. Engebretson, and the executive secretary of publications, the Rev. James R. Hawkinson, for their support in this regard.

A tributary of another kind needs recognition as well. The Rev. Dr. Egon Gerdes, under whom I started my doctoral studies, introduced me to the literature and discipline of spiritual theology. It was he who also initiated me into my area of study, classical Lutheran Pietism. He would hear himself on many pages, but particularly in regard to the interplay of the heart, the head, and the hand. The interplay of these three aspects of human life is a more graphic way of phrasing the classical monastic expression, *ora et labora* (prayer and work). Dr. Gerdes remains a primal figure in my own spiritual development.

The theme I work with is not my own. The idea that all spirituality is "a partial reenactment in our own lives of what happened once and for all in Jesus Christ as the Incarnate Word" comes from Thomas M. Gannon, S.J. and George W. Traub, S.J., *The Desert and the City* (London: The Macmillan Co.; Collier Macmillan Ltd., 1969, p.9). I have, of course, expanded and adapted it.

A word about the book. It is not a manual of spiritual exercises. It deals with a theological and experiential foundation for the spiritual life. Like life, some chapters are shorter, anecdotal, and mostly narrative. Others are longer, more involved, analytical, and reflective. In life, there are periods when we seek counsel, we read, we learn new words, we argue and trace out an idea. A scholar does this by citing and thus conversing with other writers. I invite you to overhear my conversation.

It is now my pleasure to thank Dean Robert K. Johnston of North Park Theological Seminary for his encouragement of us, his colleagues, to write. He does more. He helps to make it possible by providing support staff and by expressing personal interest. His administrative assistant, Marjorie Carlson, facilitated these details, for which I am grateful. Carol McHugh, our faculty secretary, entered this work into the word processor. She did so with grace, good humor, and care. The Rev. Mary Miller was most helpful with the section on the Lord's Prayer. My thanks also to the staff at Covenant Publications: David Westerfield, Jane Swanson-Nystrom, and Gregory Sager. These, too, are all significant tributaries. "Thank you" seems hardly enough.

Finally, to Lois, my wife, and to Clement and Catherine, my children. Sometimes those nearest are taken for granted, which is tragic. They figure in this work substantially because our lives are intertwined. The "domestic church" is a prime place for a spirituality to show its mettle as well as an environment for growth. They have helped me to know as I am known.

*C. John Weborg*
*North Park Theological Seminary*
*The Feast of All Saints*
*November 1, 1985*

TO MY PARENTS
*Reuben (†1984) and Pearl Weborg*

TO MY
*Uncle Joseph (†1983) and Aunt Florence Weborg*

AND
*Uncle Frank Weborg (†1965)*

*Since infancy they made it possible for me to
know the sacred Scriptures which are able to make
one wise unto salvation.*

# CHAPTER 1

# 'A World
# First Created'

$O$nly God has life in himself. He received it from none other. He owes his existence to no one. To have life in oneself, to be both the origin and future of life, is what it means to be God.

Human beings do not have life in themselves. To be created means to depend on the Creator for life. It is the nature of God to give life and to make life possible. When God had formed the person from the dust of the ground he breathed life into the creature. The creature was made alive—with the very breath of God. Human beings and the Divine have something in common: the breath of life. Human beings are from God and are made for God. The life with which humans are made alive is a life shared with God and with others who also have the divine breath in them. In and through God's breath we have unity with all human beings (Psalm 33:6; 104:29; Acts 17:25).

Breathing is a useful metaphor for helping one understand this life we have in common. When one breathes, two actions are required: breathing in (inhaling) and breathing out (exhaling). Many of life's fundamental activities require a similar two-fold rhythm: giving and receiving; loving and being loved; hearing and being heard; speaking and being spoken to; knowing and being known. When we breathe we show our dependence most: none of us has sufficient oxygen in ourselves by which to live. We depend on air from the outside. By breathing we are made and kept alive. And so with the other activities. By being loved, we are made and kept loving. By first being spoken to and then speaking, we are made and kept communicative. If life properly may be compared to the act of breathing, a person needs another to whom he or she may be given and by whom he or she may be received. Life is a twofold rhythm: being made alive and being kept alive.

Naturally then, it was not good that the man was alone. Without another, life's need for mutuality and reciprocal relations could not be met. The man had no counterpart to hear him, receive him, love him, and speak to him. When the woman was presented to the man there was an intuitive and instantaneous recognition: "This at last is bone of my bone and flesh of my flesh" (Genesis 2:23).

So far as I can tell, this expression is used in two ways in the Scriptures. First, in the case of the Genesis narrative, it is fundamental to the essence of human life, *blood relation or not*. We are bone of each other's bone and flesh of each other's flesh. Adam recognized that immediately. It was not just "woman" that he saw; he saw himself in and through her. Beyond each other's sexuality the man and the woman saw each other in and through each other. As Joseph Sittler has said,

> *It is precisely in the love relationship that the general enhancement of all reality has at its center a particular enhancement of myself, the lover. I love the beloved, but even more than that, I love that vision of myself reflected back to me from the beloved at ten times the normal size. I love the beloved, but even more I love that discernment of my own loveableness on the part of the other by virtue of which that other responds to me.*[1]

Paul alludes to this seeing of oneself in and through the other in Ephesians 5:28-30. There it is said that husbands should love their wives as they do their own bodies, since the one who loves his wife loves himself. Then follows: "For no man ever hates his own flesh. . . ." Is it not here implied that hatred for one's wife is at the same time self-hatred? To cherish one's wife is to cherish one's self. By implication, it is not extending the argument too far to say that hatred of another, contempt for another, any other, is hatred and contempt for oneself. After all, each and all of us are "bone of my bone and flesh of my flesh," an expression Isaiah the prophet modifies a bit and applies to one's relation to the hungry. Are you not "to share your bread with the hungry, and bring the homeless poor into your house; when you see the naked, to cover him, and not *to hide yourself from your own flesh?"* (58:7, italics mine). Neglect of the other is neglect of oneself.

Second, the expression "bone of my bone, and flesh of my flesh" does also have a more specific reference to blood and national relations. For example, when Laban met Jacob, his sister's son, he said, "Surely you are my bone and my flesh!" (Genesis 29:14). Being bone of their bone and flesh of their flesh helped to save Joseph's life when some of his brothers had wanted to kill him (Genesis 37:25-28). A political use of this term is present in the case of Abimelech (Judges 9:1,2). When David was made king, the tribes of Israel used this expression to show solidarity with the one they wanted to rule over them, using the term in a sort of national-collective sense, treating the nation as an extended family.

These scriptural references to the divine breath in each and all of us and to the common "boniness" of each and all of us is the most fundamental thing Scripture says of the human family: we are made to be *with* and *for* each other. This relational character of life is the "image of God," which image is an image of the "us" who made us (Genesis 1:26).

Even before the cross was raised on Golgotha, the cross before which we stand on level ground, there was another place, a preceding place, where the ground was level—Eden. As the papal sentence says, all human beings are guests at the banquet of life. And God sees to it that the same sun shines on all and the same rain falls on the just and the unjust alike. Whether liked or not, wanted or not, respected or not, all human beings have been made alive by the same creative and life-giving Spirit. To be a human being means to be *with* and *for* another. As it was meant to be, no condescensions, paternalisms, maternalisms, fears, threats, racial leverages, or power plays were to victimize people and put them in mortal fear of each other. The simple beauty of Genesis 2:25 creates a longing for a lost innocence: "and the man and woman were both naked, and were not ashamed." Apparently they were fearless because of complete trust. Able to look each other in the eye, free of hidden agendas and unacknowledged grievances, they were face to face, made secure in truth and love. They were *with* and *for* each other, not only physically but also spiritually and communally. Loneliness was unknown. That was the world, first created. To be spiritual and to be human were one and the same thing. To be bone of the same bone and flesh of the same flesh allowed for the distinction of male and female but did not imply separation into challenger and challenged. God's creatures were face to face. Unashamed.

What takes place when "face answers to face" (Proverbs 27:19)? In the Scriptures, the face is a well-used and powerful symbol. Most often the position or posture of the face communicated favor or disfavor. The psalmist prays,

> *May God be gracious to us and bless us and make his face to shine upon us, that thy way may be known upon the earth, thy saving power among all nations (67:1,2; cf. 80:3,7,19).*

And laments,

> *Why dost thou hide thy face? Why dost thou forget our afflictions and oppressions? (44:24).*

And reflects,

> *These all look to thee, to give them their food in due season. When thou givest to them, they gather it up; when thou openest thy hand, they are filled with good things. When thou hidest thy face, they are dismayed; when thou takest away their breath, they die and return to their dust (104:27-29).*

Isaiah speaks of God's pain at turning his face,

> *In overflowing wrath for a moment I hid my face from you but with everlasting love I will have compassion on you says the Lord, your Redeemer (54:8).*

In speaking for all, the psalmist pleads,

> *There are many who say, "O that we might see some good! Lift up the light of thy countenance upon us, O Lord!" (4:6).*

Even Paul is struck by what happens "when face answers to face":

> For now we see in a mirror dimly, but then face to face. Now I know in part; then I shall understand fully, even as I have been fully understood (1 Corinthians 13:12).

If the two-beat rhythm of life is to be maintained—loving and being loved, giving and being received, knowing and being known—face must answer to face. "Though I have much to write to you," says John, "I would rather not use paper and ink, but I hope to come to see you and talk with you face to face, so that our joy may be complete" (2 John 12). The completion of joy can hardly take place if face does not answer to face. Letters can bridge miles and intimate the feelings of the heart. Telephone calls convey a bit more intimacy than letters. One not only hears a familiar voice but also *tone* and *modulation* of voice, communicating a more perceptive intimacy. Televised telephone communication will increase the sense of intimacy because one can then see the facial expression coordinated with the tone of voice. But for all that, miles still separate the conversation partners. It may be that even with the convenience and accessibility of telephones and televised conversations, the sense of distance—while overcome in one sense—is intensified. The person that we see is present, in a way—on the screen and by voice—but not actually and any hint at his or her "being there" only kindles the desire all the more for that person's real presence. There is no substitute for face answering face, which is the fundamental posture of human beings. When we are in such a position we know instantly whether we are free or unfree in being with and for the other.

When such freedom is present we experience in that moment what God intended as the *norm* for human relations. What lies deep within all human beings is a longing for a lost innocence and an anticipation of a time when face can answer face without having to blush for sin or turn away in shame. When a person says, "I can't face him or her," he or she not only admits to a certain powerlessness but also admits to having been dehumanized, and with that, senses a keen loss of spirit. Now it seems that being human is associated with weakness, loss, longing, distrust, maybe even distaste for oneself. A sense of alienation from

God, self, and others emerges. One might say, "Whatever being human means, I do not want to be it. And since I have a hard time accepting myself as I am, what must it be for God, who does not see as human beings see?" When the phrase "face answers face" is used, it refers to being face to face, not only with each other but with God—with whom, in a curious way, we are also "bone of his bone and flesh of his flesh."

When trust is broken at any level—with God, with others, or with oneself—a part of us dies. The other, from whom we are separated, is out of reach and we are out of touch. Intimacy is gone. Isolation sets in. When face is lost, it is easy to be intimidated or to use intimidation to get the upper hand. The rhythms of mutuality then cease.

In place of intimacy there is intimidation. We feel unworthy of the other's presence and uncertain of our standing in relation to the other. Two stories will be used to show the deadly character of what happens when face can't answer face. First, from Wesley Nelson:

> Let me tell you about a sin I committed when I was about eight years old. My father had told me that I must not use some drills he had in his shop. After he had left for work, I suddenly realized how much I needed a hole in a piece of wood. The more I looked at that piece of wood, the more important it seemed to me to have a hole in it. Certainly it could do no harm. I would be very careful with the drills and be sure to put them back in their place when I was finished. My father did not really mean I should not use them. He just wanted to be sure I did not break or lose them. Then I began to think about how much I would learn by drilling the hole in the wood and how useful it would be for the thing I was making. By this time it did not seem at all like disobedience for me to use the drills. I shall never forget the terrible feeling that came over me when the drills broke. When my father returned, I stayed out of his sight. I was miserable for several days and did not go close to him. Every day I was afraid he would find the broken drill, and yet I wished he would find it so I could get it over with. When he did find it, I tried to excuse myself by telling how much I needed it, but that did not help.[2]

Second, an incident in my childhood. I remember the first lie

I told. I was quite young, and living on a farm in Nebraska. My aunt told me never to scare the chickens since it would interfere with their egg-laying habits. Well, I took a tree branch and walked into the chicken house and swished it around. Chickens flew in every direction, making quite a noise. Later that afternoon my aunt spoke with me. She had heard the noise and asked if I had scared the chickens. At first I denied it. Finally, I admitted it.

The moment was awful. It was hard for "face to answer face." I had been found out and found to be untruthful. As Paul said, "sin revived and I died."

The Scriptures contain a similar story (Genesis 3:1-7). Adam and Eve were told that they could eat the fruit of any tree in the garden except the one in the center. The tempter had come along and asked a question: "Did God say 'You shall not eat of any tree of the garden' ?"

This is a subtle point. It is not doubted that God had spoken. What is called into question is God's *motive* for speaking as he did. Ever so slightly it is hinted that God feels threatened by his creatures so he reserves a tree for himself, making it off limits to human beings. "For God knows that when you eat of it your eyes will be opened, and you will be like God, knowing good and evil."

There it is: if the man and woman eat of that one tree, they will be as God is. The very thought of it prompts God to reserve a tree for himself, alone. Furthermore, such an act, the tempter intimates, requires a defensive action on the part of the woman. "Is this the only limit God will impose? What will the next one be?" The man and woman are on the defensive.

But what happened to their view of God and his law? With regard to their view of God, he was transformed into a challenger and competitor. The gracious creator who made them alive with his breath, whose "face" seemed to have engendered no fear, was now not to be thanked but tested. As for the man and woman, trust gave way to testiness.

Next there was God's law: "You shall not eat of the fruit of the tree in the midst of the garden, neither shall you touch it, lest you die." Is this an arbitrary rule? Does it make sense to set aside one tree from use? Is this a "divine tease," something to further incite human desire? I cannot picture God acting in that fashion.

I think God's command to not eat of the fruit of the tree is similar in intent and content to Wesley Nelson's father's command, "Don't use the drills" and my aunt's command, "Don't scare the chickens." These commands are not arbitrary and they are not meant to tease us into defying the commands. They are not only reasonable, they are essential. Broken drills can't be used. Scared chickens don't produce eggs. God's command was on that order, I believe. Symbolically it stands for a proper limitation to human life, not in order to hem it in but to keep human life free and unencumbered. God's law was intended to preserve what he had made *in the condition that he had made it:* free, open, and trusting. This one prohibition sought to protect Adam and Eve from consequences they could not envision: murder, race prejudice, sexual exploitation, greed, political and economic exploitation of the poor, and so on. It was a way of showing that freedom is to be exercised with responsibility. To be free does not mean that we can do as we please. We are to do what is pleasing to God. When we do what is pleasing to God, then our neighbor is protected. This law is meant to curb any notion that freedom means self-aggrandizement to our heart's content. We are not that free. That would be a caricature of what God had intended. So if we are blessed with wealth, we are not free to spend as we will. To do so is to spend help that belongs to another in need. In many cases, it means that personal extravagance leads to the foreclosure of another's future. We are not free to do as we please, for that is not protective of the weak and vulnerable in our world.

For that reason, I have said that God's one law about the tree is a symbol of how God's law operates. It stands for whatever he has done and said to protect and preserve *what he has made as he made it.* As Paul Lehmann has said, God intended "to make and keep human life human."

My aunt's command and Wesley's father's instruction had no intention of curtailing either my or Wesley's freedom to be ourselves, to mature, or to become all that we were meant to be. There was no hint in their words of a defense of power or prerogatives. It was at that point that the tempter sowed the seeds of suspicion in Eve. He construed God's prohibition as a limitation on freedom, on human potential. When pressed about it, the woman and man fell for it. But instead of freedom they found bondage; in fact, they found out by firsthand experience what a real limitation they had become to themselves.

God was not the limiting factor. They were. How so? "Then the eyes of both were opened, and they knew that they were naked; and they sewed fig leaves together and made themselves aprons" (Genesis 3:7). It got worse. When they heard the Lord God walking in the garden in the evening, they hid. Like Wesley, who wanted to stay out of his father's sight, and like me, when I dreaded my aunt's face, Adam and Eve no longer felt comfortable with "face answering face"—with God, with themselves, or even with each other. Isolation was more comfortable but it was not consoling.

Each of us had asserted our freedom and lost it. We found out by bitter experience that what was construed as a limitation was in fact a liberation. The rule, the command regarding the tree, the drills, and the chickens was wise; it was for our good, for the good of others, and for the strengthening of the structures of life. We were not taken advantage of in any way. These rules or commands were protective of life, not prohibitive of it. If seen in this light, God's law was essential to the preservation of the created order. It was instructive as to how one should live so that the consequences would not come back to haunt, to say nothing of what might happen to others if we disobeyed. These stories help me to understand God's one prohibition. It is not a command that stands by itself. More like a symbol of all of God's laws, its intent is to keep creation as it was first made—"face answering face," with great joy and freedom. God's law was his jealous love for his creation.

Sin, then, is not really breaking rules, although that does come about. Sin breaks relationships. After I had told my lie, I knew what had happened, young as I was. I had broken a trust, a confidence. I had betrayed that confidence by not coming clean with an admission of scaring the chickens. I knew the relationship with my aunt had changed and I did not know if it was recoverable. Sin was not a private affair. It was personal but not private. Neither was Wesley's, nor was Adam's and Eve's.

Once sin had been committed, life was altered. Limitations immediately arose—face could not answer face; each of us in fact lost face. We were alive with the common divine breath, but nothing else seemed to be held in common.

Except for one thing. Wesley said, "Every day I was afraid he would find the broken drills, yet I wished he would find them so I could get it over with." And I? I saw my aunt come out of the house after I had scared the chickens. I too wanted to avoid a conversation. Yet at the same time I desperately wanted her acceptance and approval.

This is where human beings show why they are called "spiritual." This longing for "face to answer face" is a fundamental structure in all of us. This spirit transcends our self-inflicted limitations of broken faith and betrayed relationships, hoping against hope that one can be reconciled. Perhaps it hopes this because, it reasons, "If I feel a longing for reconciliation, then maybe the one I've injured longs for the same thing." This stubborn will to become one again, to reach out in hope that one is being reached for, is the primal spirituality of human beings. Sin limits. Spirit liberates. Spirit has a built-in intolerance for isolation and intimidation.

Yevtuschenko, a Russian poet of note, said that he dreamt of a "world first created," hence the title of this chapter. In order for that world to come to be, the person will have to act on what the *spirit* of the person already knows is true:

> There is no place of grace
> For those who avoid the face.[3]

The task of the next chapter is to seek understanding of what it means to call a human being a spiritual being.

## ENDNOTES

1. Joseph Sittler, *Grace Notes and Other Fragments,* selected and edited by Robert M. Herhold and Linda-Marie Delloff (Philadelphia: Fortress Press, 1981), p. 116.
2. Wesley Nelson, *God's Friends: Called to Believe and Belong,* (Chicago: Covenant Press, 1985), p. 35.
3. These lines belong to T.S. Eliot.

# CHAPTER 2

# *Fearfully and Wonderfully Made*

What does it mean to call human beings "spiritual"? Whatever spiritual is, that is what makes us human. In its primal meaning, "spiritual" is not particularly a Christian word but refers to that which is basic to all human beings. Early on, God is identified as the "God of the spirits of all flesh" (Numbers 16:22; 27:15).

As I shall use the term at this point, the word "spiritual" does not refer to godliness or saintliness. Neither does it have a particularly moral or ethical meaning. The term does not, at this point, include an extraordinary adeptness at or tolerance for spiritual exercises such as meditation, fasting, devotional reading, journal writing, or prayer. To call a person spiritual does not mean that they have an edge on these things.

"Spiritual" has also been used as a contrasting term. When used in this fashion, it is often set over against that which is "worldly," "fleshly," "carnal," or even human. Romans 8:6 serves as a classic text: "To set the mind on the flesh is death, but to set the mind on the Spirit is life and peace." When this meaning of the term "spiritual" is used exclusively, it gets set up in an either/or fashion. A person is then either spiritual or worldly.

In fact, this kind of expression leads to false thinking and false choices. The worst consequence of this mode of thinking is when people put down their bodies—even their humanity—and long to be spiritual. They fall victim to the false notion that one cannot be spiritual while being human. When used in this either/or fashion, that which is spiritual is good and is to be sought after. That which is bodily and human is denigrated.

Such sweeping judgments are not accurate and do not reflect a biblically informed mind. What God has called "good" and "very good" gets depreciated in value. The result often follows that people confuse self-denial with self-depreciation. Among the most tragic words I have heard come from people who sincerely thought that when Jesus said, "Deny yourself," he meant, "Put yourself down." Then we only humiliate ourselves. But humility and humiliation are not the same. God is not glorified and fellow human beings are not graced when self-depreciation takes over. It makes for a caricature of ourselves. Often it makes us downright unpleasant.

At this point in the discussion, then, I am not using "spirit" and "spiritual" as contrasting terms to that which is worldly or fleshly. I am, rather, picking up a theme left undeveloped at the end of the previous chapter. There reference was was made to that part of ourselves that recognizes the unnaturalness of any human situation when face cannot answer face. Whatever it is that makes it possible to know the unnaturalness of this situation is our spiritual nature. Furthermore, this spiritual capacity wants to reach out *to* another and to be reached *for*—the twofold rhythm of life. All people have a homesickness for "the world first created." The spiritual character of life reaches out *through* the body by means of speech and body language. It looks *beyond* the body, both to God and others, to be given and received as gifts, each to the other.

This spirituality, so fundamental to all of human life, can only be expressed and experienced in and through the body. Without our sensing devices—all five of them—and the remarkable neural system, how could we know and be glad that face should answer face? Yet the bodily action by itself cannot tell the whole story. Human beings can sense between words, beyond words, behind words, and in front of words that there is a person, a mind, a self that wants to be communicated, to be released, to be given to another. What T.S. Eliot has noted somewhere is true: we read between the lines to find out what one did not say. The spirituality of the human being is what makes it possible to begin to make sense of the mystery of a self that wants and does not want to communicate itself. Our spirituality takes note of the hints, pauses, oblique references, body language, and facial expression—all calculated to hide and reveal our deeper selves.

The "spirit" in the listener reaches out to identify this "extra" that seeks to get into the open. Our spiritual nature recognizes that there is always an aspect to the deepest part of our nature that cannot be put into words. Whatever that deep is can, however, be hinted at or alluded to. It is our spiritual nature that identifies with another person, so that his or her spirit knows understanding even in the silences. The Bible speaks of this as deep calling to deep. It is a call. There may be few, if any, words. But spirit knows spirit—and even the silence bears testimony. It is human spirituality that allows the twofold rhythm of life to be maintained, even when the more obvious human capabilities are inadequate. Our spirituality enables us to give ourselves and be received; to know and be known; to love and be loved. Is this understanding of spirituality at home in the biblical material? I will seek to show that it is.

God has breath. He has life in himself. What he has he gives. He breathed the breath of life into human nostrils. Human beings became more than animated organisms. They became human— alive with the breath of God and alert to their dependency on the breath-giver. This is the one "who created the heavens and stretched them out, who spread forth the earth and what comes from it, who gives breath to the people upon it and spirit to those who walk in it" (Isaiah 42:5). Possessors of breath and spirit, human beings are a unique creation. It is never sufficient to say that human beings are alive. There is an added dimension. Human beings want to know for whom to live and how this life should best be lived.

God's breath is what idols lack. They are dumb. They can neither receive nor communicate revelation (Habakkuk 2:19; Jeremiah 10:14; 51:17). As for idols, whatever is pertinent to the mind and heart is of no interest. They have no concern because they lack the breath-spirit of God. Deep cannot call to deep. They are, in the words of T.S. Eliot, "waste and void."

But the human being is not waste and void. Having been given the breath-spirit of God, human beings can be sensitized to matters beyond ordinary seeing and hearing. Deep can call to deep. The deep can come up for expression so that artists can give voice and shape to those matters that are too deep for words. Bezalel was one such person. God's breath-spirit came upon him, enabling him to beautify the tabernacle in the wilderness (Exodus 31:3-11; 35:30-35). When Othniel was selected as a judge over Israel, the breath-spirit of God came also upon him, empowering him for the task. This same breath-spirit commissioned prophets both to see what needed to be redressed in public life and to say it (Ezekiel 11:5).

By now it should be clear that to call a human being spiritual is to make a comprehensive statement. What characterizes the spiritual nature of ourselves is a capacity to know, to discern, to understand. "It is the spirit in a man, the breath of the Almighty, that makes him understand" (Job 32:8). This gift of the spirit is that which provides for discontent with ignorance and dis-ease with injustice. It is what decries anything that insults the holiness of the divine breath-giver. When the distinction between right and wrong gets blurred—when things get so bad, as Jeremiah said, that "my people have forgotten how to blush"—then people need a new spirit and heart (Ezekiel 11:19,20; cf. 18:31; 36:26). What might be the wisdom in thus speaking of both "spirit" and "heart"?

For the Hebrew, the heart was the seat of intelligence (Deuteronomy 29:2-4, AV). Sometimes "spirit" and "heart" were used in parallel lines, almost synonymously. The psalmist is a good example: "Create in me a clean heart, O God, and put a new and right spirit within me" (51:10). Bezalel the artist was mentioned earlier. The material he worked with to adorn the tabernacle came from the people who contributed jewelry and cloth. The text says that they gave with "spirit and heart." To give with the heart generally means to give enthusiastically. It means to give with understanding (cf. Job 12:3; 34:10, where heart is used in this way). When "spirit" and "heart" are put in this close

association, the implication is left that people have some awareness of what they are doing, as when we say, "I acted against
my better judgment." In some sense, "spirit" corresponds to
whatever is meant by "better judgment." It is "beyond" the
present situation and prompts questions rooted in what might
be called "criteria for judgments." "Spirit" contains a sense of
accountability and responsibility that mind does not. "Spirit" is
what tries to keep us true.

Remarkably, the Old Testament keeps this aspect ever in
view, not by philosophical reflection but in narrative form. A
common phrase refers to someone who "speaks to his heart,"
where heart can mean self. Abraham did (Genesis 17:17). David
did (1 Samuel 27:1). The fool even speaks to him- or herself
(Psalm 14:1). Hosea laments as he speaks for God, "They do not
say to their hearts that I know all their weaknesses" (7:2, tr.
Hans Walter Wolff). What might this mean?

The capacity to speak to oneself means that we can argue
with ourselves. We can rationalize an act we have done, particularly if it is questionable, to see to it that we come out on the
good side of it. We can debate with ourselves about the relative
merits of a decision needed to be made. We can interpret ourselves to ourselves, implying that we have the capacity to know
ourselves. Paul writes, "For what person knows a man's
thought except the spirit which is in him? So also no one com-
prehends the thoughts of God except the Spirit of God" (1 Corinthians 2:11).[1]

The spiritual aspect of human beings is an incredible endow-
ment. It gives us the capacity to have intuition and insight as
well as instincts. It gives us a freedom enjoyed by no other in
the created order. This freedom shows itself in at least two ways.

First, human beings can know *how* they learn as well as *what*
they have learned. This intriguing part of us is what gives rise to
learning theories: just how do people learn? It also gives rise to
teaching theories: should pupils have an open classroom, learning pretty much at their own pace, or should teaching be a
highly ordered affair? It is the "spiritual" dimension of life that
gives us a standpoint outside ourselves. Quite literally, we can
study ourselves. We can learn how we learn. Human beings are
self-conscious beings.

Second, there is another way in which we "know" ourselves. This is a bit harder to describe than the above. There we noted that we can study how we learn and how to teach. But we can use the word "how" in another sense. It has nothing to do with the *mechanics* of knowing but with the *morals* of knowing and learning. Perhaps you or I have believed something all of our lives about a certain race of people. Maybe we have a cherished interpretation of a certain Scripture text. It can be an opinion about a lot of things or a lot of people. Then we find information that challenges these opinions or views. We "know" the wrongness of our previously held views or the inadequacies of a dearly held interpretation. Some might even say, as has been said seriously, "Don't confuse me with the facts. My mind is made up." Maybe we are given to making sweeping judgments, such as I have heard made in the debate about the nuclear arms freeze, "If you hold to that, you're either a fool or a communist." Is it that simple? Are moral convictions arrived at that easily?

To engage in a deliberate misknowing or to perpetuate a dearly held prejudice or convention when the facts are otherwise is perverted to the core. The evil consequences of deliberately misknowing when we know better are incalculable. The capacity to know truly at the same time that we choose to misknow something to our advantage and to the disadvantage of others is part of our spiritual nature. To act contrary to our best knowledge for sinister and subversive "reasons" is a betrayal of our best selves, a way of "hating our own flesh," to use the language of chapter one. But at the same time, this is what gives hope to human beings. Appeal can be made to the capacity to know truly, to summon us to reconsideration, which is a form of repentance. That which keeps us open to reconsideration is our spiritual nature. There is more to us than the sum total of our thoughts, appetites, and achievements. Life is more than this. We know we are to seek another kingdom first, a kingdom where truth and love reign supreme. Our "spiritual" nature will not let us forget it. The "spirit" is a part of our mind but not identical with it. The "spirit" is what equips us to be able to keep our minds open. It also strives to help us make true judgments, not convenient ones. It belongs to the nature of the human to be spiritual.

Even the Church's liturgical life shows awareness of the spiritual character of knowing. What follows is a prayer that dates from at least 1514, although it is most frequently identified with the *Sarum Primer* of 1558:

> *God be in my head and in my understanding*
> *God be in my mind and in my thinking*
> *God be in my eyes and in my seeing*
> *God be in my mouth and in my speaking*
> *God be in my heart and in my loving*
> *God be in my hands and in my doing*
> *God be in my ways and in my walking*
> *God be at my end and at my departing.*[2]

Let us analyze it a bit. Draw a perpendicular line, real or imaginary, *after* the parts of the body named. Then draw a perpendicular line *before* the last words of each line. With the exception of the last line, the last words more or less denote an *activity* of the body parts. But not entirely. There is an "extra": the prayer asks God to be in these various parts. For good reason. While it is true that the eyes shall see involuntarily—they just do—*what* they see is more than whatever is in front of them. When some persons see Jewish people they see a reason for anti-Semitic remarks. When Ku Klux Klan members see a Black person they see those who have no place in this society. Thus, the eyes see Jews and Blacks. But they see more. What they see is what the person chooses to see. That seeing is volitional, it is willed. It's not involuntary seeing, which is the normal function of the eyes. The eyes have an inner eye just as mind has the spirit. The eyes see more than objects. They see relations. O the temptation to "mis-see." It is as real a problem as mis-knowing. The prayer invites God into the matter of seeing so that one might see as God sees. The eyes, like the mind, reflect a spiritual dimension. We see what we want to see. The gift of seeing, like the gift of knowing, is incalculable in terms of its worth and power and in terms of its vulnerability to misuse. But again, we see more than our eyes see and the objects beheld by them. The warning of a song sung by children is a worthy caution to all ages: "O be careful little eyes what you see." Inevitably, we see more than meets the eye.

Having identified the "spiritual" nature of seeing (seeing more than meets the eye) and its vulnerability to misuse, let us turn to the positive side of the issue. Because we do see more than meets the eye, human beings are able to see the world as the handiwork of God. We can behold the mystery of nature and find ourselves drawn into spiritual realities involuntarily. Before we know it, we've seen more than we've seen! Alertness to the hidden glory is mandatory.

Some years ago, together with my family, I was riding up Pike's Peak on the cog railroad. As we neared timberline, the conductor asked us to notice the small pine trees. They grew in bunches of two or more. The reason for this was that, at that altitude, subject to harsh wind and weather, they needed each other for protection.

My imagination was sparked. I saw more than two or three trees clumped together. I looked through a window on all of life. I asked a question: "Does this mean that, at bottom, all of life is social and communal and that even nature outside of the human family bears witness to this reality?" Survival cannot be seen as the heroic act of one person. Somewhere and sometime someone enabled the other.

My hunch received support from reading the noted biologist, Ashley Montagu. He wrote, "No living organism is biologically solitary in its origin and few are solitary in their lives."[3] Looking in a microscope then and seeing the "communal nature of cells" one sees more than a biological speciman. One sees a sign of the entirety of life. Solitariness as such is not there. Reality is social—botanical, zoological, human. We do not, of course, see in the specimen or in the trees a proposition: reality is social. We see more. The hint, the suggestiveness, the mystery of interdependence—all of these point to life that is beyond the specimen and the trees. Our "spiritual" nature can thus see, envision, describe, and be awed by the grandeur of this world.

This power to see more than meets the eye is what also makes us creators of a world in which to live. The Scripture speaks of God who "makes all things new." To make something new means that we can see and imagine what the "new" might look like. Let us consider these narratives about "world making," about making all things new.

The *Chicago Tribune* of August 7, 1985, carried a story about two teachers in the Chicago public school system. Joyce Oatman teaches at Crane High School, where the valedictorian of the class of 1979 scored 9 out of a possible 36 on ACT tests. Dipping into her savings account and prevailing upon some of the best teachers, Oatman formed Crane Academically Able Program (CAAP). The teachers worked extra hours and on Saturdays. This year twenty-eight of CAAP's thirty-two seniors have been accepted by various colleges. Oatman's personal statement shows the power and imaginative prowess of the "inner" eye, that which sees more than what meets the eye:

> *I came up with the idea of a holistic honors program, some-thing that would not only make the kids smarter but would also socialize them, change their work-ethic, make them like school and teach them something about morals, so that the girls wouldn't be getting pregnant and the boys wouldn't be out stealing.*

Monica Zabor, at age sixty-seven, is an English teacher at Austin Community Academy. She has taught there for twenty-one years, having begun her career at age forty-six. Her special attention, along with four other teachers, is on the task of keeping seventy-seven students with low reading scores, failing grades, and a yen to cut classes from dropping out. This program is so tailored to the needs of students that they get prere-corded wake-up calls at home. This alertness to ghetto prob-lems and home situations partially explains her view that teachers are three persons in one—parent, teacher, and preacher.

> *Kids will open up to you at the strangest times, and one should be able to sit down and listen without regard to [the] bell or a schedule, because you might not have another chance to do it again.*

Then she added,

> *I began to realize the power that a teacher has. I find I had a real skill to define what it is an individual student needs. It was as if I could read his mind.*

Oatman and Zabor saw more than meets the eyes. True, they saw the conditions that limit and inhibit learning. But they also saw that they could condition the very circumstances that stifled the education of the students. What did they see? They saw stu-dents as fundamentally *responsive* persons. Students are not hard as rock and dense as fog. Students do not live in an impenetrable world. They can be engaged. Oatman and Zabor saw themselves as entering the debilitated and distressed world of these students. They trusted that if students knew of their trustworthiness, of their care and not just curiosity, they would open up to them, and allow them as teachers, as authority figures, into their lives.

Oatman and Zabor were persons of profound self-understanding. Apparently, nothing was beneath their dignity. One dipped into her savings to fund this extra effort, this journey into the lives of the disenchanted. The other went so far as wake-up calls—to high schoolers at that! But above it all was an alertness to indicators that were not yet put into words: "I had a skill to define what it is an individual student needs." Recall Eliot: " . . . listening between the lines for what you didn't say." Here deep cries out to deep.

Oatman and Zabor had a fundamental conviction that human beings are responsive. What makes us responsive, even when we are most resigned to a situation, is our spirituality. Sometimes our spirit has to be awakened, lured, or led out of its dormancy. It looks for something to energize it. The two teachers did that with concrete actions: after-hour tutoring, any-moment listening, morning wake-up calls. A spirit gets communicated in, with, and under these very mundane activities. That is why, at the beginning of this chapter, I tried to show that spirit requires body. Spirit gets from one person to another by means of hands, gestures, gifts, words, eyes, ears, telephone calls, and so on. Spirit requires body—physical means to get itself across to another. The other has the equipment to receive and decode these signs. We have already noted how often Scripture says that she or he "spoke to her- or himself." Perhaps these students asked, "Why all this effort for me?" "Why are these people concerned—even using their own money for my sake? They don't have to." A transition then occurs. The focus shifts from "them" to "me." "Am I worth their time?" "Do they think that much of me?" "Should I think more of myself than I do?" So it goes.

It is possible for disenchanted students to become enchanted with themselves. They could even begin to imagine themselves differently. This happens when someone else gives them new eyes. Note, now, the sequence. The students began to see *themselves as they were seen.* They began *to know themselves as they were known* and *to love themselves as they were loved.* All of this came about in very ordinary ways. Do not overlook the ordinary. That is to overlook God's way.

Human beings are fearfully and wonderfully made. We have powers that are unique in the creation. We are not *fated* to an environment. A tick is with its three senses. It is sensitive to light, smell, and changes in heat, so when a warm-blooded animal goes beneath it the sensors tell it to fall on the animal. The tick cannot diversify its place, rethink anything, or find a new place in the world.

We as human beings are *fascinated* by our environment. We are lured into studying it, painting it, and writing about it; yet we have still not exhausted the lure. Ticks are aware of only one segment of the world. Human interest is universal and we can identify with persons in other parts of the world, rejoicing with them in good fortune and lamenting with them when they are victimized. Because we have this capacity, even space and time do not prohibit a sense of presence *with* and *for* these people. Human beings transcend location. We recognize that face wants to answer to face because we know, we just know, that we are bone of each other's bone and flesh of each other's flesh.[4]

It is our spirituality that has endowed us with the capacity for fascination and has freed us from being fated to anything. Spirit and freedom go together. They presuppose each other. Because of spirit, human beings are reachable. Neither give in to fate nor give up on anyone. Death to the spirit is death to the self. "Quench not the Spirit," either God's or your own (1 Thessalonians 5:19, AV).

## ENDNOTES

1. For expanded exegetical treatment of the themes in this section, see: Walther Eichrodt, *Theology of the Old Testament*, 2 vols., tr. J.A. Baker (Philadelphia: The Westminster Press, 1961, 1967), II:131ff.; Hans Walter Wolff, *Anthropology of the Old Testament*, tr. Margaret Kohl (Philadelphia: Fortress Press, 1974), chapters 4 and 5; George Carey, *I Believe in Man* (Grand Rapids: William B. Eerdmans Publishing Company, 1977), pp. 26-31; Ray S. Anderson, *On Being Human: Essays in Theological Anthropology* (Grand Rapids: William B. Eerd-

mans Publishing Company, 1982), Appendix A. For a New Testament study, see C.F.D. Moule, *The Holy Spirit* (Grand Rapids: William B. Eerdmans Publishing Company, 1978), chapter 2.

2. For a brief study of this prayer, see Frank Colquhoun, *Prayer That Lives* (Triangle: S.P.C.K., 1981), pp. 20-22.

3. Ashley Montagu, *On Being Human* (New York: Hawthorn Books, 1966, 1950), pp. 30-31.

4. This section has been informed by two works, Wolfhart Pannenberg, *What Is Man?*, tr. Duane A. Priebe (Philadelphia: Fortress Press, 1970) and Jürgen Moltmann, *Man*, tr. John Sturdy (Philadelphia: Fortress Press, 1974).

# CHAPTER 3

# *Love the Questions*

Wolfhart Pannenberg says that all human beings experience a "pressure to the open." We want freedom and know that we are made for it. But that presents a problem. We can get ourselves into trouble. Wesley Nelson did when he used the drill bits. I did when I scared the chickens and lied about it. Adam and Eve did. While all of us got ourselves into trouble, none of us could get ourselves out of trouble. We experienced a "pressure to the open," a persistent longing to be on good terms with those whom we had disappointed and disillusioned. We once knew the freedom and settledness we had had before we had committed our misdeed. Now we were unsettled and unfree but we could "imagine" the situation when freedom and settledness could be restored. We were living, as Augustine has said, between memory and hope. Our memory (of the good times) informs our hope (for the good times to return). By remembering, we are inspired to retrieve what was lost, renounced, or just frittered away. We know what we want. We sense a "pressure to the open," that which keeps hope for better times alive. This "pressure to the open" is what the previous chapter has tried to describe as our spirituality.

When intimidation replaces intimacy with God and others, persons are on the defensive. They know that they *want* reconciliation ("pressure to the open"). They do not know if they dare to approach the other and ask for it. And here is where the two-beat rhythm of life needs to be communicated clearly. The persons who have been disillusioned, distressed, deceived, and disappointed by the other need to send signals that are worth the while if the offender is to approach and ask for understanding and grace. Remember: all of us have the equipment to "speak to ourselves" as the Scripture says. We have the capacity to be fascinated with the signals we send each other. None of us is fated to alienated living. It is not in the cards that grievances must become grudges. Hostility is not fated to become hatred.

We are made for face to answer face because we are bone of each other's bone and flesh of each other's flesh. When we have turned away from each other's face, we need some way of being turned around. It needs to be shown that it is worthwhile to do so because we know that we cannot free ourselves. Whomever they are that we have disregarded or deceived, it is only they who can free us. It is not within our power to do so. How they go about freeing us is a key point. How do they take advantage of our "pressure to the open"? How do they get us to "speak to ourselves" about these things?

In mid-August of 1952 I was struck with paralytic polio. I was fifteen years old, ready to enter my junior year in high school. I was paralyzed from my hips down. At one point I had virtually no feelings in my feet. For some time I had to wait out the infectious period. No drug would stop the infection. One also waited to make sure that the paralysis had finished doing its dirty work, and had localized. I was fortunate. My lungs suffered no paralysis. Neither did the upper part of my body. But what I did suffer was more than enough.

After the infection had ceased and the paralysis had localized, hot packs were put on the legs and therapy was begun. First, the muscles had to be loosened, then strengthened. It was dreadfully painful.

One Sunday morning two of my doctors came in. Therapy had been in progress for a while. One of them said to me, "John, do you want to get out of bed?" While asking the question, each of them got on one side of me and helped me to sit up. Then gradually they eased my feet to the floor. Feeling had returned. My feet tingled and felt funny. My legs had no strength. Were it not for the strong support of the doctors I would have collapsed. They put me into the bed. One of them said, "Thank you. I'll see you tomorrow."

At this time I had studied no philosophy. Most fifteen year olds have not. The doctor's question, "Do you want to get out of bed?" did not register as anything profound or even provocative. I did no sophisticated analysis as to its possible meaning. Meaning would have to await its time.

Some eighteen to twenty years later the time for meaning had come. I was a pastor in Princeton, Illinois. I was preparing my Sunday sermon on the assigned gospel text, which was a healing miracle. In it Jesus asked a question as in John 5:6: "Do you want to be healed?" I had a flashback to the fall of 1952 and the remembrance of a question, "John, do you want to get out of bed?" Now it made sense to analyze the question. It was intriguing.

I noticed that my doctor had not asked, "John, do you want to walk?" The very use of the word "walk" would have promised more than he could have assuredly delivered. It was not known at the time whether I would ever walk. His question appealed to my spirit, not just my reason. Reason alone might question any possibility at all. What the doctor appealed to was that which transcended reason and made me open to possibilities that were not yet evident. I noticed that the doctor's query was *interrogative in form* but *indicative in mood.* It led me to a more technical formulation: "The *inquiry,* 'Do you want to get out of bed?' is really an *indication* of possibility that you might walk." An inquiry became an indicator. A hint sought to become a hope. He appealed to that part of me that could see beyond what is. Thus hope began to structure and support the will. The question became my quest for locomotion and made it possible for me to see myself as something other than a paralyzed victim.

My experience prompted me to read the Bible in a new way. I had never paid any attention to the questions God asked of people in the biblical narrative. But now these questions have become all-important. I will use a selection of the questions and comment on them in light of what I learned from my polio experience.

Genesis contains the story of the flirtation with temptation and of how Adam and Eve fell for it. Then they knew shame for the first time. They hid from each other behind fig-leaf clothing. They hid from God behind the trees. Face could not answer face anywhere. Now it was more comfortable to be unknown. But it was not consoling.

A voice is heard. A question is asked: "Where are you?" Response: "I heard the sound of thee in the garden, and I was afraid, because I was naked; and I hid myself." The voice: "Who told you that you were naked? Have you eaten of the tree of which I commanded you not to eat?"

Notice that the first two questions are indirect. The first question cannot be answered "yes" or "no." It is indirect in form, but very directional as to purpose. "Where are you?" In order for Adam to answer it, he must find out where he is in relation to God, Eve, and himself. The question puts him squarely between memory and hope. Furthermore, the question is not meant to embarrass him but to enlighten him. The second question shares the same mood and form: "Who told you that you were naked?" There is no "yes" or "no" answer. But Adam's "spiritual" nature is fully taken advantage of by God. A human being has the capacity to rethink his or her life. Our "pressure to the open" knows the wisdom in doing so. Only on the basis of such reconsideration can one's life be reclaimed. The questions help us to know ourselves as we are known. They have the earmarks of revelation. We are drawn into the open.

If we have had the courage to open up our lives to the questioner, then we are prepared for the third question. It is different in form. It is direct. "Have you eaten of the tree of which I commanded you not to eat?" Now notice: God did not begin with direct questions. They come across as accusations. They close off one's "pressure to the open." Such initial directness often embarrasses people more than it enlightens them. First, God showed his understanding of their situation by being indirect, though not indecisive. He did not crowd Adam. He gave Adam space and time to hear and own the question. But God let the questions do the work. The questions gave Adam language with which to "speak to himself."

What were the questions intended to do? They were to indicate that God was truly interested in Adam and Eve. They were to demonstrate that he knew more than they thought he knew. But they also were to show that God would not use this knowledge against them. These questions were a way of drawing Adam and Eve to face God, each other, and themselves. God had initiated the conversation. By that he had indicated that he was as dissatisfied with the situation as they were.

Let it be observed that God's questions were *interrogative* in form but *indicative* in mood. God indicated his alertness to the plight of Adam and Eve. Furthermore, the inquiry, "Where are you?" was an indication to them that their isolation could end. Intimacy could replace intimidation. Questions have an uncanny way of making people come to life.

A second divine interrogation provides another example. Genesis 4 tells the story of Cain's murder of Abel. Even before the murder God anticipated something askew in Cain's heart. Cain's offering to the Lord was not acceptable. Note God's query: "Why are you angry, and why has your countenance fallen? If you do well, will you not be accepted? And if you do not do well, sin is couching at the door; its desire is for you, but you must master it." Take note: the questions begin indirectly. Every opportunity is given for Cain "to speak to himself," to know himself as only his spirit knows what is in him. It is a chance to reconsider life and redeem it. The question is intended to give time by forestalling hasty action. Cain was confronted. But he was not crowded.

Then he murdered Abel. God returned with a question. Notice its indirectness: "Where is Abel your brother?" The next question, "What have you done?" does lead to specifics. The pattern of this compares well with Genesis 3: God proceeds slowly, indirectly, indicating by the questions that he is available to hear the story. He gave Cain space and time.

The story of Jonah provides another example of the divine genius. Jonah has to be regarded as one of the most effective evangelists in history. He preached to the city of Nineveh, enemies of his own people. All of the inhabitants, including the king, repented. God had mercy on them, including the cattle!

Jonah was mad. ". . . I knew that thou art a gracious God and merciful, slow to anger, and abounding in steadfast love, and repentest of evil" (4:2). Now these were God's people, to the consternation of the reluctant prophet. His eyes could see nothing more in Ninevites than Ninevites. His inner eye could not see them as God's own nor as his fellow believers. His mind could not conceive that such was even possible!

God comes to Jonah. Twice in chapter 4 God is noted to have asked, "Do you do well to be angry?" It is a perceptive question. In order for Jonah to answer it, he had to deal with three matters: the unresolved tension between his people and the Ninevites (i.e., he must overcome political justification to perpetuating hatred); his own unwillingness to see in the Ninevites anything but enemies; and, finally, he had to deal with a God who is free to love whomever he wills.

The questions are gentle and full of grace. They address the spiritual capacity in human beings to be opened up to a new self-understanding and a new understanding of God. When Jonah is confronted by God's freedom to love the Ninevites he has a chance to glimpse the meaning of that same freedom toward him. Nothing forced God to turn his face toward Israel. God's question pinpoints the fact that his freedom is the basis of the gospel of grace. Questions, when properly processed, have a way of making us both alive and alert.[1]

Jesus was a master user of questions. In Mark 2 there is a description of Jesus' healing of a paralytic. Jesus had also pronounced forgiveness of the man's sin. Some Pharisees objected, saying that Jesus had blasphemed God—since only God can forgive sin. Notice Jesus' first question. Its indirectness invites a reconsideration of the accusations against him: "Why do you question thus within your hearts?" When one observes that this was said to a hostile group, one immediately notices the wisdom of the question. It is indirect but very intentional. It creates an opportunity for reassessment and for rejoicing with a person having been made well in spirit as well as body. The title of Bruce Larson's recent book comes to life in this episode: *There's a Lot More to Health Than Not Being Sick.* Jesus' question opened that horizon to his detractors, seeking to offer the same wellness to them. He had hoped that they might have seen his point.

On another occasion, James and John said to him, "Teacher, we want you to do for us whatever we ask of you." Talk about a blank check! Jesus: "What do you want me to do for you?" James and John: "Grant us to sit, one at your right hand and one at your left, in your glory." Jesus: "You do not know what you are asking. Are you able to drink the cup that I drink, or to be baptized with the baptism with which I am baptized?" One question asked by Jesus let these disciples hear themselves talk! Did they truly hear themselves? Jesus gave them every opportunity to hear that their request was not just for favoritism but that it was subversive to the community. In fact, if Jesus had acceded to their request he would have *supplanted* the community of the twelve with a community of two. His question was for their enlightenment, not embarrassment. Those who have ears to hear, let them hear (cf. Mark 10:35-40).

Just think of the power in Jesus' question to the man who had been paralyzed for thirty-eight years: "Do you want to be healed?" (John 5:6). Or to Judas on the night of the betrayal: "Judas, would you betray the Son of man with a kiss?" (Luke 22:48).

Questions can quicken. That is their grace and power.

Let us move the scene from the biblical material to the present time and show how questions still function in powerful ways. Let us also recall the title of the book: *Alive in Christ, Alert to Life.* Properly framed, questions have a way of making the attentive listener come to life. Maybe even one should say, "come to his or her senses." At the same time, questions require alertness to what is going on, to the questions implicit in a given situation. I recall an occasion when Dr. Eric G. Hawkinson, former dean of North Park Theological Seminary, observed, citing a Swedish historian, "It is important to know what is happening in what is happening."

Suppose you receive a phone call from a teacher of your high-school child informing you of an incident in school involving angry and potentially destructive behavior. Let us also note that the teacher expresses a genuine interest and is not vindictive. Your child comes home. You might have said, "Well, you really did it today, didn't you?" Or, if damage was done, you might have said, "What did you do that for?" Note how both are accusatory in language. The questions are *interrogative* in form. In mood, they carry an *indictment*. Furthermore, the parent puts distance between him- or herself and the child. Little room is given for dialogue, for the child to reveal anything of a personal nature.

Change the form of the question. "Did you have a tough day at school today? I had a phone call from the teacher that would indicate so." Notice the absence of indictment and accusation. The use of the word "tough" allows room for dialogue, for the child to tell a story. The distance between parent and child is reduced and in fact, the parent can be drawn into the story so that the child knows that the parent is a part of his or her life *and* a part of the future of that situation.

This form of the question also shows that the parent has identified in some fashion with the child. When we identify we indicate an *interest* in the person and an *intention* to be for him or her in a significant way. Thus, the second form of the question is *interrogative* in form but *indicative* in mood. To the extent that there may be parental embarrassment, it is not allowed to alienate parent from child. To the degree that there is disappointment, the relationship is not allowed to disengage. One question can open or close a relation. The natural "pressure to the open" can be facilitated or it can be stifled, thus making the child more uptight than ever. "Pressure to the inside" can only lead to a blow-up.

Questions are not always as explicitly stated as in the above incident. Sometimes they are implied in a situation. When that is the case it takes an alertness on the part of the person to recognize them. But they are there, noticed or not. Some time ago I heard of parents to whom a highly deformed child was born. Many operations were required. Extended hospitalizations were the rule, not the exception. As I recall it, the parents said that their first question was, "Why us?" It reflected the utter inability to explain this event, to say nothing of the frustration and pain present.

Time went by. They came to recognize, they said, that that was not the only question to be asked. Another one came to mind. They had the courage to ask it: "Why *not* us?" The new question had not answered the old one. It shed little or no light on "Why?" But the new question helped the parents move into a new way of relating to the situation. What emerges now is a growing sense of solidarity with people who live in similar circumstances. Perhaps there is a lessening of the feeling that "something is wrong with us; that's why this happened." Along with that, a greater freedom may develop to embrace the child and themselves, *as they are.* One need not be other than one is: questioning, committed, hurting, vulnerable. In any case, a question helped these parents move into a zone of freedom. Having accepted themselves, they were freer to be accepting of others and to be available to others in similar circumstances.

A third instance. I come from the farm. Weather is fickle. A neighbor can have a crop virtually destroyed by hail. One's own might remain untouched. Numerous responses are possible. One is, "I'm lucky." A second, tinged with arrogance says, "God must be favoring *me.*" Another is, "This is a mystery but I am profoundly grateful." When one asks, "What does this mean?" one is hard-pressed for an explanation. The question cannot get an answer. It can get a response, the same kind of response one has when grace has been offered instead of a judgment one probably deserved. In those circumstances grace is unexpected and unanticipated. Hoped for? Perhaps. Expected? No. But there is no explanation in those cases, either. The experience of being fortunate when misfortune abounds all around is no testimony to what we deserve, as if God were indebted to us or that we had a claim on God.

Alertness to this "mystery in the ordinary" is another window on the mystery of grace. Grace has a way of keeping one humble. So does the experience of being fortunate. Be alert to life. Alertness to life will make one aware of God's ways, hidden to the proud but revealed to the humble and receptive. Should it not also be the case that the most fortunate of people in these cases should also be the most generous?

In the writings of Rilke there is this counsel: "Learn to love the questions. Someday you might live yourself into the answers." Notice the relation between learning and loving. People need to show hospitality to questions that come their way. Hospitality, like love, gives more than passing attention to guests. Guests are invited into one's home. They are "entertained." Love, like hospitality, gives time and space to the recipient of its attention and affection. In this setting of love, hospitality, and attentiveness, we learn to know our guests and they learn to know us. When guests sense genuine love and hospitality they reveal more of themselves. What is *learned* from them is conditioned by our *love* for them. Without love, learning is curtailed before it starts.

The questions in life that make a difference need to be loved. Their significance will not be known without hospitality being shown to them. The really profound questions need to be loved if they are to teach us anything. It takes real courage to give hospitality to the question of a child who asks, "Daddy, do you have to be gone again tonight?" It is one thing to live with the question. That is painful. It is probably not productive. It is just endured. But when one *lives* the question one has begun to identify with the questioner and to share the concern of the questioner. This can also be painful, but this pain is more like pain on the way to healing. There is commitment to the truth and justice of the question and to an alteration in the situation. These questions turn into guests. We become companions of the "question-guests" and they take us into new territory. In specifically Christian vocabulary, this is the meaning of conversion.

Whenever a question about the direction of our lives comes along, there is a tear in the surface of life—a tear, a rip, an opening.[2] The classical Christian mystics referred to this experience as a "wound of love." The surface of life gets opened. At the initial stages, we are passive. The question comes along and makes an opening. We are opened whether we like it or not. We do not dictate our children's questions, nor our spouse's, or our life's experiences. We are torn. We are wounded. We can give hospitality to these experiences or not. In any case, we will not learn anything without at the same time loving them.

The asking of questions is no small matter. Strictly speaking, the questions being asked are not about the abstract category, "life." They are about one's own life in the process of living it. It may be about a life that should have been lived, might have been lived, or yet could be lived. The grammatical mood is the subjunctive. Wistfulness pervades the entire process.

Philosopher Charles Winquist suggests that these "wounds" or "tears" be called "the middle of experience."[3] Note: the middle. It happens before things are over and done with. Because the questions arise in the "middle experience," time is given for one's life to be reconsidered. One can go back and recollect the history of one's life. One can also imagine a more satisfying life. As we have already noted, it is our spiritual nature that allows us to live between memory and hope. This is truly, "the middle of experience."

Precisely then what do questions do? Why should we be alert to the questions? How do they make us alive? Questions help us to go back. They help us locate where things went wrong. And when. And how. In this process of *reopening* one's life history and of being *open* to what one comes across, a creative moment occurs. One learns that if one can "live the questions" which are asked, the boundaries of one's life are torn away and made open to new possibilities. We are not fated to whatever situation we are in. Winquist says that "the ability to question maximizes the field of experience." This is the direct result of our spiritual capacities. We can ask beyond and behind any horizon of our lives. We have eyes to see what is not yet visible but can become so.

When we become "companions of the guest-questions" the field of our experience is maximized and, as Winquist also says, "everything is touchable by the reality of the question." Just take the child's question, "Daddy, do you have to be gone again tonight?" The question can maximize our experience by enlarging it to other relations—to one's spouse, to God, to oneself. When we allow the question to maximize our experience, we soon learn that it has the potential of reaching into all our experience. This "tear" or "wound" in the surface of life has the potential of opening a large aperture. But while this is so let us be comforted in knowing that the same child who asks the question is the one who loves us and wants our love. The same God who inflicts a "wound of love" is also the physician who offers "the oil of gladness instead of mourning" (Isaiah 61:3).

As I said at the outset, we cannot redeem ourselves. The questioners and the questions are our companions. They can open us to that which redeems so that in the end we are not alone with our sin and loneliness. "Learn to love the questions. Someday you might live yourself into the answers." The "middle of experience" has the potential for being a most fruitful time of life. Questions leave no part of life untouched by their inquiry. But if followed, the minimums of life can be avoided. Hospitality, then, to the questions![4]

# ENDNOTES

1. There are other similar instances in the Old Testament. Look at God's interchange with Abraham and Sarah in Genesis 18. Consider God's conversation with Jacob in Genesis 32. Ezekiel 37, Job 14, and Isaiah 50 provide equally fascinating accounts of careful and creative use of questions.

2. Paul Tillich makes creative use of this metaphor. See *The Shaking of the Foundation* (New York: Charles Scribner's Sons, 1950), chapter 7. See also Charles Winquist, *Practical Hermeneutics: A Revised Agenda for the Ministry* (Missoula: Scholars Press), pp. 41-43.

3. See Charles Winquist, *Homecoming: Interpretation, Transformation and Individuation* (Missoula: Scholars Press, 1978), pp. 15-17; see also *Practical Hermeneutics: A Revised Agenda for the Ministry,* pp. 3, 27, 29, 30, 33, 55-57 and 59.

4. I first learned this language from Henri Nouwen, *Reaching Out* (Garden City and New York: Doubleday and Company, Inc., 1975), chapter 4. On the more precise relation between love, knowledge, and learning, see Parker Palmer, *To Know As We Are Known: A Spirituality of Education* (San Francisco, et al.: Harper and Row Publishers, 1983), chapter 1.

# CHAPTER 4

# *Life Is a Journey*

*L*ife is a journey. Like life itself, a journey has an inner and an outer aspect. My grandfather emigrated from Sweden to the United States. That was the outer journey. It could be measured in terms of miles and hours. The various modes of transportation could be named: ship, train, and wagon.

But there is also an inner journey. It began in Sweden. He had to say "goodbye" to family, friends, and land. The place to which he was going was an unknown, except for an uncle living in Illinois. He didn't know the language, the customs, the expectations. At a more profound level, he was going from being a citizen (in Sweden) to becoming an alien (in the U.S.A.). This journey was from the known to the unknown, from the familiar to the strange, from the old to the new. Once he had arrived in the U.S.A., he went to Illinois to work for his uncle in order to pay off the debt he incurred when the uncle had paid for the boat ticket. Following that he married, began to raise a family, and started farming. Later he moved to Nebraska and after some years, successfully ran for the state senate. A neighbor once said to him, "John, we don't mind you foreigners coming out here to farm but we don't like your getting into politics and telling us [i.e., 'natives'] what to do." He was still stuck with being an alien despite his naturalized citizenship.

The two aspects of one journey go on simultaneously. The one is external, the other is internal. Our lives have a landscape and an inscape. The inscape, I have a hunch, is the most vexing. One can arrive at one's destination outwardly (in my grandfather's case, America and the Great Plains) only to discover that at deeper levels one is not there at all. There are some who choose to see others only as aliens, intruders, and undesirables.

Virtually every minority knows this experience. The destination outwardly is America. The inner destination is freedom. Very frequently, the inner destination is never reached. What America promises is elusive. A dream dies. These people know by heart what the proverb means: "Hope deferred makes the heart sick." The landscape is beautiful. The inscape is a desert.

Let us try another narrative for the sake of emphasis. Take the case of a person just discharged from a hospital for the mentally ill. Let us also suppose that the hospital is in the town where the patient lives. The journey home may be only three miles and the landscape may look familiar to the patient on the ride there.

But the inscape is another matter. The destination is more than home, although that is the place to which the patient is going. The real destination has to do with people as much as place. Will the neighbors really accept me? How will my family relate to me? When I sit in the pew at church, what goes through the minds of those who sit next to me? This is the inscape the person sees and hears, and this journey is not over when the patient arrives at the front door of his or her house. In a way, that journey begins in earnest when "face answers face," and the patient "speaks to him- or herself" about the meaning of these things. He or she is looking behind, in front of, beneath, and beyond the words for signs of acceptance on which to anchor hope. It is one thing to *go* home. It is quite another thing to be *at* home. Others grant that or withhold it.

I have found it helpful to use a diagram. The left perpendicular line represents the outer, the external journey. This includes the experiences, the most common to the most exceptional, such as one's birth, first day at school, a death, first job, and so on.

The right perpendicular line represents the inner journey and includes the "marks" the outer experience leaves on the human spirit. These are the things we speak to ourselves about. I let each hash mark represent an experience or perhaps a cluster of experiences. On the inner journey, each hash mark represents the mark left by the outer journey.

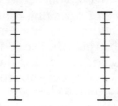

Let us turn this into a spiritual exercise and see what insight it might offer. I will use my own life as an example:

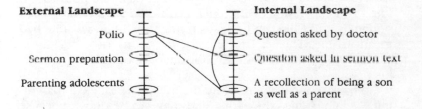

**External Landscape** — Polio — **Internal Landscape** — Question asked by doctor

Sermon preparation — Question asked in sermon text

Parenting adolescents — A recollection of being a son as well as a parent

I have already made substantial reference to my encounter with polio and the profound experience that it was. You will recall from an earlier chapter that my doctor's use of questions eventually led to a new way of reading Scripture. But you will recall that many years separated my sermon preparation, when those questions came to life, from the event in the hospital. Thus a later event retrieves, recalls, and makes possible a reconsideration of previous events. In my diagram above, I use lines to connect events. By this means I can begin to integrate my experiences and to let them be drawn up into the larger mystery of God's ways. It is also a way to name one's experiences, to own them, and to put them in a larger providential context. When these experiences are left unnamed, especially when we know their content, we are less than honest with ourselves. And when honesty is hard to come by, so is hope.

Let us try another example. Take note of the hash mark on "parenting adolescents." That is an interesting age. Parents often feel taken for granted. You are just there at the beck and call of kids. The two hardest words in the English language for them to say seem to be "thank you." And so it goes.

For me, this experience of parenting caused me to retrieve, perhaps reactivate, a relation with my father that had been allowed to lapse. When I had polio he learned physical therapy in order to get me walking again. He did this for well over a year. But as often happens, it takes one experience to recall another. So, while reflecting on the ease with which kids omit "thank you," it came to me that I had never told my father what he meant to me; nor had I told him "thank you" for all of his sacrifice of personal time during my recovery from polio. The problem was that when it came to me during my experience of parenting, my father was somewhat into senility so that he could not process ideas and expressions with much clarity. So I wrote him cards on family and Christian holidays trying to tell him what he had meant to me. Thus, a later experience of my own put me in touch with an important but unfinished aspect of my personal history.

Go back to the diagram. Note the hash mark labeled "parenting." Again, some connecting lines have to be drawn because the experience of being a parent brought to mind that I was also a son and that there was a relationship with my father that needed to be completed. And with that, it once again becomes clear how one experience overlaps the others, penetrates them, and shapes them.

But note also that as we attend to what we know about ourselves, take it seriously, and act on it, we can have integrated lives. When we are honest with ourselves we also bring hope to ourselves. Naturally so. Our lives get straightened out as they get simplified. This is not to promise a trouble-free life. It is to encourage a journey inside, our attentiveness to the inner self in order to see what needs attending to and what needs to be acted upon.

The word "member" may serve as a root word for three

other words, each of which is very descriptive of the journey of life and its effect on us: dismember, remember, re-member.

Life has a way of *dismembering,* of separating us physically, psychologically, and spiritually. We sense a distance, not only from others but from ourselves. These separations are by no means always deliberate. The ordinary journey of life pre-empts the attentiveness we should have given to significant others. As a character in Eugene O'Neill's play, *Ah, Wilderness!* says, it's "the pace that kills along the road." People who have been significant just get crowded out. The pace goes on. Little attention is paid to what is being lost. Until, that is, an experience comes along and one *remembers.* That is what happened to me. I was made alert to my neglect of my father by noticing the effects of the "pace of life" on the relationship between my children and me. Nothing at all malicious. Just the ordinary pace of things. Yet the alertness that came made it possible for me to be made alive. That is where the third word enters. After remembering what was, what ought to have been, and what can be, one can begin to *re-member* what had been dismembered.

It is our spiritual nature that makes this possible. We can "speak to ourselves" about these things. We have already taken note of Augustine's helpful observation that we live between memory and hope. We thus remember in order to re-member. God comes to us with his questions in the midst of "the living of these days," as Fosdick termed it.

God's question to me was, "What does it mean to be a son?" The question placed me between memory and hope, an advantageous position indeed, for by remembering I could begin the task of re-membering what had been dismembered by "the pace that kills."

Tragically, if we do not use the journey of life as a journey into the caring and creative task of re-membering, we may end up with the tragic view expressed by a character in one of Donald Barthelme's short stories. He notes how today's view of life is that of the insurance adjuster. An adjuster comes after the tornado has struck, after the fire is out, after the accident has happened. What such a person sees is roofs separated from houses, fenders from cars, and limbs from people. Dismemberment is all around.

By contrast, Christians believe in atonement. Interesting things can be done with hyphens. Note this: at-one-moment. This suggests doing what the insurance adjuster cannot do: re-member. But it is the Christian's vocation—with God, self, and others. Treat your hash marks as guests. Let them open you to hope by way of memory.[1]

A journey also involves space and time. We want to know how far something is and how long it takes to get there. Just as the journey through life entails an inner and outer aspect, so the journey through life entails an inner and outer sense of space and time. These are spiritual as well as physical dimensions. They have to do with our place, not just on a map but also in relation to others. When God asked Adam, "Where are you?" it was a question of location which is a matter of space and time.

In 1979, my family and I were on a trip to Colorado to enjoy some narrow-gauge railroading, and to Arizona to visit the Grand Canyon. It was my first sustained experience *in* and *with* the desert. The "wide open spaces" became just space. There were no towns, water towers, landmarks, or anything. There were sand and rock formations but they were not landmarks. One gets oriented by one's relation to landmarks. One can move closer to them. Space can be measured by miles, shrinking miles at that. Time can be measured by hours and minutes. But not in the desert. The horizon is not fixed. It moves as one moves toward it—no closer to it, no further from it. That is just the opposite of landmarks. They are fixed. Clear dimensions of time and space result.

But that was not my experience in the desert. In the desert I found a sense of motion without movement. I was conscious of being in relation to nothing; there were no limits, no sightings, no fixed points. Even a sense of direction was hard to come by. When there are no limits, no landmarks, what are you east or west of? Nothing was present to mediate a sense of place, of location, to me. One meaning of space is that it represents what is between, e.g., between the door and me. The door is a reference point and mediates a sense of location to me. In the desert, I knew none of that. I had a sense of being lost in a space that was between me and nothing. To be lost is to have no relation to that which can let you know where you are.

By contrast, let us look at my boyhood experience on the farm where I was raised in Nebraska. Landmarks abounded. The Tyrrell family lived across the road. There was a clear, almost tangible sense of space (how far) and time (how long to walk the distance). When I was plowing or cultivating the field on the north side of the farm I could see the water tower of Pender, my hometown. It was a landmark. Seeing it I knew I had a relationship. It located me. I was three miles away (space) and about six minutes (time) from it. In relation to the Tyrrells and to Pender I had a clear sense of movement from or movement toward. In both cases, a clear sense of the "between" existed.[2] Contrary to my experience in the desert, there was no sense of a vastness that seemed to get larger the farther one went. The contrast between these two experiences come down to this: in the midst of nothing, the only thing that remains is an indefinite sense of time. It can be frightening.

After some reflection on these experiences I formulated four sentences:

1. An infinite sense of space creates an indefinite sense of time.

2. We overcome time by overcoming space. When a sense of space is lost, time takes over.

3. There are two kinds of space: a true between, and just plain vastness.

4. By creating a visible sense of space we create a viable sense of time.

How does this apply to the spiritual journey? I will use two occasions from life and one from the Bible in order to illumine my point.

Reconstructing from memory, I recall an article by a psychiatrist whose practice was with college dropouts from a prestigious eastern school. Over a period of interviews he discovered, along with another physician who had similar patients, that the fathers in the homes of these dropouts spent on the average of thirty-five seconds a day with their children! The students came from families of high achievers. Expectations, demands, almost performance quotas existed as in business. Furthermore, dad paid the bill, so produce! But thirty-five seconds a day. It is enough time to give a lot of demands. Such short periods of time are ready-made for curt responses and abrupt sayings. But it is not enough time to develop relations, to show interest, to invest oneself in one's child, to hear a child out in a discussion. It is time enough to put a child down. That is what happened. The children felt the demands. They did not feel the devotion. Consequently they had no staying power when the chips were down. Authority figures were resented because they were never experienced at home as being supportive or as being present. All they ever left were demands.

In these cases, a significant landmark was not around during the days of youth. The child felt an infinite distance between him or her and the parent. The parent might have been around occasionally, but it is one thing to be present; it is another thing altogether to be present *for* the child. That takes time, trust-building conversation, and just plain companionship. But you see, in this case, the father *gave* no time to the child. The parent *took* time away and created a sense of infinite distance between himself and the child. Can you imagine the tension growing up when the most significant people in your life have no time for you? Nothing puts distance between parent and child more quickly than that. Then children have to take time into their own hands, go their own way, hoping to find that landmark to whom they can relate.

When parents give no clear sense of relation to their children, they create a desert experience for them. An infinite sense of space creates an indefinite sense of relational time. There is nothing viable in this sense of time because the parents have no time to show interest in their children. Because the basic capacity to wait for fulfillment in life is learned from parents who keep their word to their children, the children who have thirty-five-second-a-day parents develop no waiting capacity. There is no one to show them faithfulness and patience. Children then take time into their own hands. Careless eating habits, undisciplined minds, often promiscuity, and little endurance follow. They are old by the time they are thirty-five. Instant gratification becomes their mode of life. When it does not come about, there is rebellion. Without a true experience of relational space they have no viable sense of time. In order for a child to have a proper sense of time, he or she needs a true sense of relational space. For that, one needs a landmark to mediate the location. Parents are that landmark.

Let us shift from a family setting to a church setting. No church escapes the painful problem of people who quit attending. Often they are not contacted by representatives from the church until after a long period of time. As I have heard it said, the church representatives are greeted with the question, "What took you so long? I thought no one even missed us."

What do church people often say when these persons are mentioned to them? "Give them a little time. It will work out." Or, "It will take care of itself. Time heals." There is enough truth in those lines to be hopeful. There is not enough truth to be helpful.

"Give it time." What's an "it"? The very impersonality of the pronoun makes it sound like we are waiting on an impersonal process and not serving people. Change the saying to "Give time to them." That is another story. Let us not be fooled. Time will not take care of it unless we take care of time. Nor is it really true that time heals. Time by itself hardens. Truth by itself hurts. Time, carefully employed, and truth, caringly told, will provide the conditions for healing. When we draw near, we give time. The longer we stay away the more time we take away.

Churches create desert experiences for their people when they "let them be," hoping that in time the people will forget what happened and return. Churches, in the person of representatives, must become landmarks, clearly visible signs of interest and care. If people are ministered to *when* they distance themselves, they know that the church has drawn near to them, created a sense of "between," and has given them time. This visible sense of relation creates a viable sense of time. In any case, the first task is to create a sense of space, to let people know they are still in relation. Then people know they are given the time in which to process the tension. Time becomes grace and leads to hope.

Let us turn to the Bible. We have already looked at the questions God asked in Genesis 3. Now I want to pursue them from a different perspective.

After the man and woman had sinned they sensed a great distance between themselves and God and each other. The space seemed infinite. Trust had been broken. The relation "between" seemed lost. There were no landmarks. When space is infinite time gets to be indefinite. Could anything be worse than perpetual alienation? The man and woman were in sight of each other but the distance seemed infinite.

Then God broke in. He began to ask questions. He had shown himself. By initiating a conversation, he created a sense of space, of relation. A landmark was now on the horizon. By creating a sense of space he broke the tyranny of time—of isolation in perpetuity. This "visible" sense of space made for a viable sense of time.

When time is given, people can relax. They know there is a space in which they can reconsider their lives. They do not have to take time into their own hands. Time is now both a gift and a task. It can be used to reconcile, to reconsider, to repent. God made himself accessible, creating a zone of freedom for a man and woman who wondered if it was at all possible to get back in God's good grace. By his grace, perhaps, they could then create a visible sense of space and a viable sense of time for each other. Space and time are divine gifts. Let us redeem the time by creating a proper space in which persons can live and move and have their own being.

In order to create a proper space for people, great discernment is required. People cannot be forced into conversation. Love and grace are often difficult to receive, let alone give. Hardness of heart and hopelessness of spirit are often eased gradually and require both space and time. Those who offer love and grace cannot put the recipients on their own timetable. Nor can those who show care force God into their own wishes for a quick and easy solution. God knows the proper spiritual pace for people. We must trust God's timing, loving people gradually into wholeness. Speed kills. I have formulated the following guides for myself.

1. Always maintain a distinction between *caring* for people and trying to *cure* them. Caring for people allows one to vary the closeness and distance of the relationship as is appropriate. Trying to cure them turns one into a messianic kind of figure. It relies more on power than on presence.

2. Be *motivational* but not *manipulative*. The former has a way of igniting faith and hope. The latter too easily violates the

freedom of the persons being helped and turns them into objects of power.

3. Be *intentional* but not *intimidating*. The former allows for the initiatives of grace and the integrity of steadfast love. The latter too easily shows disregard for the pace of spiritual recovery. Trust is built slowly and experientially. One must give time in order for trust to have the time to mature.

4. Be *nourishing* but not *nagging*. The discernment here calls for knowing when it is time to pull back, to enlarge the space, so that the person does not fall victim to spiritual overcrowding. When that happens, people feel that their freedom is being taken from them. They may even feel that the person helping has a greater need to succeed than he or she has genuine interest in the persons being helped.

5. Know the difference between being *conscientious* and being *compulsive*. Persons who are compulsive in their relations to others act as though they have no faith that God will act. They tend to do God's work *for* him instead of *with* him. Their intensity and swiftness tends to create problems because those being helped become defensive. A curious dynamic gets set up. The more compulsive and pushy the helper becomes the more resistant and slowly the one being helped responds. It is a ready-made situation for alienation.

The next chapter suggests a model for the spiritual life. At its heart lies a patient, confident waiting, based on the assurance that God in his own way and in his own time will vindicate not only his Word but the confidence his servants have in the divine promise. It is that promise that keeps us faithful at all times—persistent, perhaps, but never pushy. And the mystery of the spiritual life lies precisely in waiting for God to show himself at the time he knows best. This will become evident in the story of Jesus' journey to Jerusalem.

## ENDNOTES

1. Try this method of Bible study. Pick out a journey-story. Make the two sets of lines representing the outer journey and the inner journey. Draw hash marks representing the outer and inner events. Then try to see how the events interconnect and how one event can recall and retrieve another, giving it new meaning. An extensive and challenging story to work on is the Joseph narrative, Genesis 37-50.

2. I was alerted to the profound meaning of "the between" by reading Martin Buber's *Between Man and Man,* tr. Ronald Gregor Smith and the Introduction by Maurice Freedman (New York: Macmillan Paperback Edition, 1965). Consult especially p. 203.

# CHAPTER 5

# A Model for the Spiritual Life

*C*hristian people have had a fascination with saints. One of the reasons this fascination persists is that saints always appear to be larger than life. They are capable of miracles, of superhuman endurance, of an indescribable depth of love, and of a wisdom beyond telling. Sometimes their actions are legendary. We smile but we go on reading books like Butler's *Lives of the Saints, The Little Flowers of St. Francis,* Foxe's *Book of Martyrs,* or the *Martyr's Mirror,* a staple devotional book among the Mennonites. Technically this is called "hagiography"—the study of the writings of or about the saints.

Saints are to Christians what heroes are to the general public. Heroes also appear larger than life. Sports heroes break each other's records and make it into the *Guinness Book of World Records.* Jackie Robinson is a hero, not just because of his baseball prowess but because he broke the color line in professional baseball. By doing so, he became another kind of hero—the one who makes equal access to opportunity a bit more of a reality. Helen Keller is a hero to thousands of handicapped people. Both Robinson and Keller as heroes and Polycarp and Bonhoeffer as martyr-saints are larger than life. And that is precisely what God's grace does: it makes an ordinary human being larger than life. In doing so, it makes that person a living demonstration of God's power.

Scripture, like the Christian tradition and like ordinary people, speaks of examples to be followed. Paul speaks of "the example of the faith which our father Abraham had. . ." (Romans 4:12). Paul said, "Be imitators of me, as I am of Christ" (1 Corinthians 11:1). The writer of the book of Hebrews says, "And we desire each one of you to show the same earnestness in realizing the full assurance of hope until the end, so that you may not be sluggish, but imitators of those who through faith and patience inherit the promises" (Hebrews 6:11,12). But most prominent of all is the example given us by our Lord Jesus Christ. As Peter writes, "For to this you have been called, because Christ also suffered for you, leaving you an example, that you should follow in his steps" (1 Peter 2:21). The imitation theme reached a certain popular height in the United States with the publication of Charles Sheldon's book, *In His Steps*. A saint, a hero, held up for imitation is one way to find a model for one's spiritual life. But it is not the only way.

My own model is an event. I do not claim it to be better than others. It expresses my own need for a model by which to explore the mystery of the Christian life, particularly when that life is understood as a network of relations: to God, to myself, to others, to institutions, to time, to location, and so on. Relations have the character of an event. They have a beginning. They ebb and flow. They can become dormant and they can be renewed. And besides, I need a way of accounting for God's providential care, his surprising works of grace, and his periodic withdrawals. With regard to my own person, I also need a model that can join the active and contemplative aspects of the spiritual life so that both aspects, prayer and service, are formed and informed by the other. The event that best helps me explore the nature of the spiritual life is the transfiguration of our Lord.

First of all, and in keeping with a motif of this book, the transfiguration occurs mid-point in the journey of Jesus from north to south, from Galilee to Jerusalem. This journey is more than a geographical trip. It is also an inward journey. The closer Jesus gets to Jerusalem the nearer he gets to his death. This is the profound mystery of Jesus: he is to give his life as a ransom for many (Matthew 20:28; 1 Timothy 2:6). This inward journey is a journey from glory—the ministry of miracles and power—to suffering—his willingness to bear in his body the sins of humankind (Hebrews 9:28). The journey from north to south is experienced inwardly as the journey into his vocation as the Suffering Servant. As Lutheran theology might put it, it is a curious paradox: the glory of Christ is his cross and his cross is his glory. Even the Apostles' Creed commends this "curiosity": Christ descends to the lowest portion of the earth—death and Hades. No place is too low for him to be (Psalm 139:7-10; Ephesians 4:9,10). No person is too far out for him to be with them (Luke 19:10). He knew how to be humble and how to be humiliated—with grace! And yet, he was no one's doormat! The glory of Christ is his cross and his cross is his glory.

Second, the transfiguration occurs in close proximity to the first announcement of Jesus' suffering at Jerusalem (Matthew 16:21-17:13; Mark 8:31-9:13; Luke 9:18-36). Note the juxtaposition: the prediction of his death and the manifestation of his glory! I have called this the mid-point. I am not arguing that this event bisects Jesus' ministry when it is exactly 50 percent done. No, the transfiguration occurs in the middle of experience, where experience comes to a head, where a threshold is crossed. The mid-point is the critical point, the point of opportunity for utmost creativity. Jesus created a most curious paradox: the glory of his life was found in his cross; the cross in his life was formed to be his glory. Thus the transfiguration is the mid-point in two journeys—geographically from Galilee to Jerusalem and internally from glory to suffering.

Third, liturgical matters come into play. By the fourth century the Day of Transfiguration was celebrated in the East and by the ninth century it is known in the West. It was formally declared a universal feast by Pope Callistus III in 1457 and ratified by appropriate synods in the fifteenth century. But Luther was not satisfied with the date of August 6. The reason he found this date inadequate was that it did not fit the story line of the Bible. If the transfiguration marked the first passion announcement, then, if the Church was to keep it as a festival part of the unfolding drama of the history of salvation, the celebration of the transfiguration should make the end of the season of glory, which is Epiphany (which means "manifestation" or "a showing forth") and the beginning of the season of suffering, i.e., Lent.

Luther preferred to celebrate this day on the Sunday preceding Ash Wednesday, which is also the last Sunday of the Epiphany season. A look in the back of *The Covenant Hymnal,* in the section covering the Church year and the texts assigned for preaching on those days, will indicate the Covenant Church's harmony with this practice—which is also consistent with that part of our heritage which has its origin in the Lutheran tradition. In this fashion the worship life of the Church maintains the tension of the glory of the cross and the cross of glory. This tension has a way of presenting itself to us in the middle of our experience, where thresholds are to be crossed, questions turn into lifelong quests, and vocations are truly owned. The journey leads to Jerusalem, where, in the crucible of life, one's commitments are revealed and offered to the Father for his vindication in due time.

Now let us turn to the transfiguration itself. It has already been noted that it occurs in connection with the first announcement of Jesus' suffering and death. As for the internal journey, it is the middle of Jesus' experience—the dividing line, the point at which his life takes its decisive turn.

> *Now about eight days after these sayings he took with him Peter and John and James, and went up on the mountain to pray. And as he was praying, the appearance of his countenance was altered, and his raiment became dazzling white. And behold, two men talked with him, Moses and Elijah, who appeared in glory and spoke of his departure, which he was to accomplish at Jerusalem. Now Peter and those who were with him were heavy with sleep but kept awake and they saw his glory and the two men who stood with him. And as the men were parting from him, Peter said to Jesus, "Master, it is well that we are here; let us make three booths, one for you and one for Moses and one for Elijah"—not knowing what he said. As he said this, a cloud came and overshadowed them; and they were afraid as they entered the cloud. And a*

*voice came out of the cloud, saying, "This is my Son, my
Chosen; listen to him!" And when the voice had spoken, Jesus
was found alone. And they kept silence and told no one in
those days anything of what they had seen (Luke 9:28-36).*

First of all, the transfiguration narrative, like the narrative
describing the baptism of Jesus, is dependent to some degree
on Isaiah 42. When one turns to that text, one is immediately
struck by the expressions that appear in the narratives of the
baptism and the transfiguration. One notices immediately the
expression "my chosen in whom my soul delights" (Isaiah
42:1) as having affinity with "my beloved Son; with thee I am
well pleased" (Matthew 3:17; Mark 1:11; Luke 3:22). Furthermore, the chosen one of Isaiah 42 is a recipient of God's
Spirit—the power to do the will of God with heart, mind, and
soul. This same phrase, "my Chosen," appears in the transfiguration narrative (Luke 9:35, cf. Matthew 17:5; Mark 9:7). Thus,
two significant phases of the Lord's life are introduced by the
same words, "my Chosen in whom my soul delights;" the ministry of glory, which began with his baptism, and the ministry
of suffering, which began at the transfiguration. True, these
should not be read as absolute separations, for, after all, the
baptism was to fulfill all righteousness and the one baptized was
the Lamb of God who was to take away the sins of the world
(Matthew 3:15; John 1:29).

What is worth noting is that this one Old Testament text
undergirds two primary narratives. These narratives come at
the beginning and in the middle of Jesus' life and work. This
repeated use of Isaiah 42 suggests that the two phases of Jesus'
life—postbaptism and posttransfiguration—bring out two very
important dimensions of his own spirituality and service. Each
segment is introduced by using the same text, thus assuring the
followers of Jesus that the one who started in a blaze of glory
and ended in a deserted death is the same one God had chosen.
The glory and the cross belong together and find their vindication in the Father.

Second, Isaiah 42 blends two dimensions of the Servant's life
and work. On the one hand there is a very *personal* ministry, a
ministry to the weak, the doubtful, the powerless, the ones
who can lay claim to nothing and who, in turn, are claimed by

no one. These persons are called "bruised reeds" and "dimly burning wicks." These are the people who at times are carried by others and they themselves carry no one. They are more conscious of the pain *of* life than a purpose *for* life. To these persons, the Servant of God is a "wick-turner-upper"! Neither a sophisticated nor scientific term at all, it nevertheless denotes the patient task of nurturing hope in people, of awakening a sense of worth, of building trust and therefore a ground for hope. Faith usually acts in hope upon the receipt of grace. It is not so much caused as called forth. Much of the time, this is interpersonal, often one to one.

On the other hand, there is a very *public* dimension to the Servant's work. Notice how often the term "justice" occurs (Isaiah 42:1,3,4). Here the concerns of the Servant shift from the interpersonal needs for hope and love to the public concern about those structures, institutions, and systems that deprive people of a sense of worth, of hope, and of vigor. The Servant becomes a voice for those who have none and a symbol of those who live on the margins of life. The Servant takes the concerns of the "bruised reeds" and the "dimly burning wicks" and makes them his cause. The marginalized people now have a representative who is unashamed to call them brothers and sisters. There is, in the apt word of the Polish people, solidarity.

My own view of spirituality requires the blending of the active and contemplative dimensions, the personal and public, and the priestly and the prophetic. In yet another set of terms one might speak of the spiritual and the sociological. By using the story of the transfiguration I can employ both sets of terms in what for me is a creative spirituality that exhibits itself in the world. Now, back to the event of the transfiguration (Luke 9:28-36).

Jesus takes Peter, James, and John up the mountain in order to have a season of prayer together. Is it any wonder! The full brunt of his journey to Jerusalem has now been acknowledged. It is appropriate at this point to recall another expression from Isaiah 42: "He will not fail or be discouraged till he has established justice in the earth. . . " (v.4). In some segments of the early Church, much attention was centered on the problem of discouragement. It was no small matter. When speaking of this particular syndrome of spiritual dis-ease, some of the Christians referred to it as sloth. But this word may not be immediately helpful because it brings to mind an ugly, three-toed animal, or just plain laziness. While laziness may accompany a "slothful" spirit, that was not the heart of the matter. What really was of concern was that sloth meant that one makes despair the criterion of a lifestyle. Hence some early writers come close to making despair or sloth a major source of sin while we in Western Christianity, almost without thinking, make pride the chief cause of sin.

While this is not the place to debate whether primacy of place belongs to pride or despair, it is worth noting that at what must have been a very low point in his life, Jesus does not want to pray alone but in company. He does not want to fail or be discouraged until he has established justice in the earth. A tall order! From his friends he acquires perspective on himself and on his vocation, just as he had done before the triumphal entry into Jerusalem, when he went to the home of Mary, Martha, and Lazarus (John 12:1ff.). In the mysterious economy of things friendship has a way of strengthening fidelity, and belief has a strong connection with belonging. Jesus does not pray alone. He prays in fellowship.

As he is praying, two people appear to talk with him, Moses and Elijah. What does one make of this? An obvious association links Moses with the law and Elijah with the entire prophetic vocation of making the law relevant to specific situations. The relation to Jesus? For one thing, he himself had said, "Think not that I have come to abolish the law and the prophets; I have come not to abolish them but to fulfill them" (Matthew 5:17). Later in his ministry Jesus identified the great commandment as loving the Lord God with all of one's heart, soul, and mind and one's neighbor as oneself. Then he added that on these two commandments hang all the law and the prophets (Matthew 22:37-40). He certainly had embodied the legal and the prophetic tradition in his own life. Is it not the case that he had loved God with his heart, soul, and mind and his neighbor as himself? Could we not then be over and done with this text by simply saying that all that had been hoped for had now been fulfilled in Jesus and that the transfiguration was the revelation that this indeed was the case? What more could one want? The situation is almost psychedelic. Light is all over the place. His countenance changes. His clothing dazzles with whiteness. The entire scene is alive with divine disclosure. Even a voice is heard, "This is my Son, my Chosen; listen to him!"

For all the power that is in this scene, I seek more. While reading the account of Moses' life, a new vista on his role was opened. True, he is the lawgiver. Maybe even Jesus is the new Moses and the Sermon on the Mount constitutes the new law, as some contend.

But beyond these more formal comparisons there is another dimension in Moses' life that compares with the work of Christ. In Exodus 32:30ff., an encounter between Moses and God is described. It takes place after the golden calf has been built and after Moses had broken the tablets of stone on which the commandments had been written. All of this had been done in hot anger. But then Moses is mindful of the peoples' sin. They are threatened with expulsion from the book of life. Moses asks God to take his name out if it is impossible to forgive the sins of the people. Moses even speaks of his intentions to make atonement, perhaps by offering his own life as the text might suggest. Now what is this but a *priestly* act? All kinds of words cluster about. Moses' act: representation, sacrifice, substitution, expiation, and so forth. In fact, the psalmist celebrates this priestly act of Moses (99:6 and 106:19-23). The priestly service of Christ about to be accomplished at Jerusalem is in fact the topic of conversation between Moses, Elijah, and Jesus. They speak of his "departure, which he was to accomplish at Jerusalem" (Luke 9:31). The priestly work of Moses is somewhat of a paradigm for the priestly work of Jesus. For he too will offer himself, the one for the many.

Elijah was a prophet. There was expectation that he would appear before the great and terrible day of the Lord dawned (Malachi 4:5). Even the populous had suspicions that Jesus might have been such a prophet (Luke 9:19). Elijah had had a very public ministry. He had raised the dead (1 Kings 17:8ff.). He was outspoken in his critique of the political system (1 Kings 18:17ff). He also had "passed on" his spirit to Elisha (1 Kings

19: 19ff.). Jesus himself had pointed fully to Elijah's ministry in his sermon at his home synagogue in Nazareth (Luke 4:16-30). He began the sermon by reading from Isaiah:

> *The Spirit of the Lord is upon me,*
> *because he has anointed me to preach good news to the poor.*
> *He has sent me to proclaim release to the captives*
> *and recovering of sight to the blind,*
> *to set at liberty those who are oppressed,*
> *to proclaim the acceptable year of the Lord.*

This text is remarkable for what it leaves out in the quotation from Isaiah 61:2. Jesus omits the reference to vengeance. This is not because he disbelieves in God's eventual judgment. It is rather because this good news must first reach all of the captives, the blind, the poor, and the oppressed. Remember Isaiah 42:4: "The coastlands wait for his law!" This is the year of the Lord's favor upon those who have learned to expect no favors whatsoever. Life is not full of surprises for those who have learned to expect no favors at all. It is the same old thing —blood, sweat, and tears. Or as another biblical text has it, "There is nothing new under the sun" (Ecclesiastes 1:9).

But prophets not only speak of the new; they sometimes bring it. Elijah did. In this text in Luke 4, Jesus says that there were many widows in Israel in Elijah's day, but it was to a widow in Zarephath in Sidon that he went. He raised her son. There was something new under the sun brought from an unexpected source at an unexpected time. Prophets occasion the new because they identify with those for whom nothing is new. It was said that the Jews had no dealings with the Samaritans. Jesus did. It was new and the potential fallout from that act was nothing short of breathtaking (John 4:9ff). Elijah and Jesus had begun to penetrate the coastlands and God was making all things new.

Prophets are an endangered species. They bring to mind what others try to forget. They are a voice for those who have given up speaking—like Rosa Parks in the early stages of the civil rights movement. When asked to move to the rear of the bus to go where she "belonged," she let it be known that "she would not be moved." A voice. A slogan. She knew it all too well: if one is moved regularly, one is eventually moved out of everything, which is exactly what prejudice wants to accomplish. Prophets are killed for their witness, as was Jesus. The popular idea is that if the prophet, the leader, is killed, one can also silence the problem. But the scheme does not work when there is a resurrection. God does not permit his holy one to see corruption.

My model now begins to take shape for me. Might it not be the case that on the mount of transfiguration what is truly revealed is the priestly and prophetic character of Jesus Christ, the combination of Moses and Elijah, the spiritual and the sociological, the personal and the public? This of course stems precisely from his having kept the law in every respect, fulfilling in both personal and public fashion the love of God and neighbor. But the subtlety of this must not escape us. From a human perspective, it was his *prophetic* lifestyle that got him killed. But when his life was taken from him, he prayed even for those who killed him. He gave them the benefit of the doubt since in his prayer he told God that they did not know what they were doing (Luke 23:34). This is also a point that Paul takes up in his first sermon, recorded in Acts (13:27). This intercessory prayer and personal sacrifice for the undeserving is his *priestly* ministry. As it stands written, "For Christ also died for sins once for all, the righteous for the unrighteous, that he might bring us to God . . ." (1 Peter 3:18).

The prophetic and priestly dimensions stand in a healthy tension. The priestly character stands in, with, and under the prophetic. It keeps prophecy from turning into demagoguery. The prophet is not a hit and run artist. The prophet is in solidarity with his or her people. Their concerns become his or her cause. The disenfranchised know this. So do the oppressors. They do their best to break this bond, to kill the hopes of people by killing the one who speaks for them. So the prophet, while preaching judgment on the oppressors, prays at the same time for their salvation. The word of the law is intended to bring them to their senses by bringing them to Christ. In this way the priestly work of the prophet is carried out and the prophetic work of the priest finds a proper form. Apart from Jesus Christ, this combination is beautifully but tragically present in the life of Stephen. This first martyr, upon being stoned for his witness, gazed into heaven. Upon seeing God's glory and Jesus standing beside the Father, he prayed, "Lord, do not hold this sin against them" (Acts 7:60).

At this point my theology tells me I am missing something. I have identified the prophetic and priestly character of the Lord's life and work. Theology done in the Reformation tradition says that one more aspect needs to be added—namely, the kingly. But it is hard to find a kingly aspect here. There is no third person to represent this aspect. Perhaps the light and glory suggest something regal. But all this talk of dying on the cross does not bespeak such a throne. The talk is about a departure, not a coronation. I grant the mystery, but at the same time I think there is a kingly aspect somewhat hidden in this event.

As yet, we have not done much with the voice—the voice of the Father who identifies Jesus as his Chosen One and the One in whom his soul delights. All of this is said prior to, and in preparation for, Jesus' death. It appears to have made little or no impression on the disciples. They want to locate on the mountain and build three booths. The journey to Jerusalem is so far from their interest. Maybe the thought of the inward journey that would inevitably result from the outer journey to Jerusalem was just too threatening.

But Jesus hears the voice. It is his only consolation. For now, communion with the disciples seems to have been somewhat broken. In order to keep from failing or being discouraged (i.e., fall prey to sloth), Jesus now has communion with the Father only, something perhaps like the sustenance Elijah received from the ravens when only they could bring him bread and meat (1 Kings 17:1-7). The voice in a curious way is a personal crowning of Jesus before his public exaltation, which he received at the ascension. Before he goes to Jerusalem, before the intense suffering starts, Jesus is assured of his Father's blessing and vindication. His cross and his glory are drawn together. His glory will not prevent his cross, and his cross will not tarnish his glory. Both will be revealed in one act. Before the time, Jesus receives his vindication—although this vindication will only become public after the resurrection. All Jesus has is the voice and the words it spoke. But then had he not said at one time that no one lives by bread alone but by every word that proceeds out of the mouth of God (Matthew 4:4)? Now he, like we, would have to live and die by this word.

It is well, then, to consider how some of the early preaching of the apostles treated this matter of the resurrection. In Peter's sermon on Pentecost he speaks of Jesus as having been killed by lawless people. Then he says, "But God raised him up . . ." (Acts 2:23,24). After having healed a lame man, which provided an occasion for a witness, Peter said, "The God of Abraham and of Isaac and of Jacob, the God of our fathers, glorified his servant Jesus, whom you delivered up and denied in the presence of Pilate. . . . But you denied the Holy and Righteous One . . . and killed the Author of life, whom God raised from the dead" (Acts 3:13-15; cf. 4:5-12, 5:27-32, and 13:26ff. for other examples). What is significant is the continual recurrence of the proclamation that God raised him. It is God who vindicated Jesus, in his own way and his own time. There is the interval between Good Friday and Easter morning. Intervals are important. There is always an interval between planting and harvest, between a thesis and its proof or disproof, between invention of a new product and its marketing. Vindication of the effort is not immediate. There is waiting, perseverance, and patience.

Paul was aware of this, too. In a poetic text full of the proclamation of the Gospel, Paul elaborates the theme of Christ's humiliation and God's exaltation of him. In Philippians 2:5-11 he asks his hearers to have the same mind as was found in Christ. He did not consider equality with God something to be hoarded but instead emptied himself and took on himself the form of a servant and became obedient unto death, even death on the cross. This much Christ did: he humbled himself and made himself vulnerable to the supreme sacrifice. What did God do? God highly exalted him, giving him a name above every name. It is God who raises the dead. It is God who exalts. It belongs to the Father to vindicate the work of his Son done in obedience to his will. To have the mind of Christ means more than just having a willingness to be humble and to be a servant. This mind is also keenly aware of the Father, who vindicates and exalts *in due time*.

Paul also spoke of this divine vindication regarding himself. He writes, "For we do not want you to be ignorant, brethren, of the affliction we experienced in Asia; for we were so utterly, unbearably crushed that we despaired of life itself. Why, we felt that we had received the sentence of death; but that was to make us rely not on ourselves but on God who raises the dead . . . " (2 Corinthians 1:8,9). The key element here, as in the transfiguration narrative and in the Philippians 2 passage, is the work of the Father in exalting and vindicating his servant. That is the royal element, the coronation, the annunciation that our God reigns—in his way and in his time.

I need to illustrate how this might work in real life. I have a story in my files, the source of which is lost, of a certain Robert J. Cronin of Chicago. He had made it in the eyes of peers and associates—a successful business, a stable and happy family, membership in a country club, and other attributes of the upper-class. He became aware of those who had no idea of his kind of life because they lived in the housing projects with little access to the more creative and celebrative side of Chicago. He made himself available to the Cook County Department of Public Aid to try to help the more than 20,000 fatherless children and their mothers who lived in just *one* of the projects.

What did he do? First he found a way to get a school bus to use and then secured a bus driver's license. He took thirty to forty boys to the zoo, to night baseball, and to Lake Michigan. Then he took them to steel mills, airports, etc., to try to instill a sense of the opportunities in life and the need for education and training.

But his interest was not limited to occasional trips. As his relationship with these thirty to forty boys deepened, so did his sense of vocation toward them. Once-a-week trips, important as they had been, were not enough to affect the direction of their lives. So he began to bring them out to his home where his own family could participate and provide as familial setting. All of this was new to the boys. His wife and daughters taught them painting. A son got them started in athletics. Even music was taught. Tutoring was done and report cards were examined as if they were the cards of Cronin's own children. Prizes were given for high marks. A climate had been created for achievement. Cronin even helped some with the education beyond high school. Such a bond of affection had been created that when one of Cronin's daughters was married the boys insisted on buying her bridal bouquet.

But not everyone in the neighborhood rejoiced with such a generous spirit. When the neighbors saw thirty to forty black children show up every Saturday they got riled up. It happened in Cronin's neighborhood as Boris Pasternak says happened in Jerusalem during Holy Week: "The alleys crept with sly whispers." And more. The neighbors burned a cross on his front lawn and made threatening phone calls to his family.

Cronin was undaunted and undefeated. Patiently he helped the neighbors understand his vision and some even caught it. Some of the boys took a neighbor's brain-damaged child for a wheelchair ride each weekend. Likewise, Cronin helped the boys work through a very painful experience in race relations.

How does this fit my model? For one thing, Cronin exercised a very public and prophetic role. He certainly identified himself with a group that lived on the margin of life. They were just "contained" in the projects. They had access to very little that could have enhanced their chances for a productive life. Furthermore, there was solidarity with them. When the neighbors acted against him he did not break off his relations with the boys. If anything, it became stronger. Prophets belong in communities.

For another thing, he exercised a priestly function. He went to those who tried to do him in, even by threatened violence. Recall T.S. Eliot's lines:

> There is no place of grace
> for those who avoid the face.

Cronin turned his face toward them, offering in a face-to-face encounter the possibility of reconsideration and reconciliation. It was a courageous and caring move. Thus, while his prophetic act stirred up hostility, Cronin's priestly act offered hospitality even to those who were hostile. Like Jesus and Stephen, his attitude seemed to be one of giving his neighbors the benefit of the doubt: they knew not what they had done.

But how does the kingly operate here? Simply in this: Cronin had no idea when he began how his efforts would turn out. He had no guarantees of being appreciated or even received. Maybe he did not think that his friends would turn on him and that for a while, at least, his only solidarity was with his family and with those who could not do a thing to help him. No doubt it was his family who kept him from failing and being discouraged—that is, from falling victim to sloth, to despair as the criterion of a lifestyle. Someone else had to vindicate Cronin's work. And in due time, there was a harvest. But not without an interval of time and the interruptions of suffering and false accusation. The crowning of the effort comes later and in unexpected ways. And in the cases of some people, the crowning of their efforts has been after their deaths. It is in God's time and in God's way. The kingly belongs to God.

So there is my model for the spiritual life, illustrated by a true story. It combines the active and contemplative, the priestly and the prophetic, the spiritual and the sociological. It helps me to serve without demanding results. In spiritual things, results are given, not demanded. Results are gifts, not possessions. I am their steward, not their owner. I am called to be prophetic and priestly and to wait for the king to crown the efforts in his time and in his way.

The next chapters become more analytical. By the use of theological and liturgical materials I seek to show how the mystery of Christ—his life, death, and vindication—holds promise for us as we live our lives in Christ. In order to do that, attention needs to be given to language, ritual, and concepts as they not only inform our minds but actually shape each of our lives into a "little Christ."

# CHAPTER 6

# *Spirituality: What Are We After?*

*T*he norm of prayer is the norm of faith or believing (*lex orandi, lex credendi*). This ancient formula teaches that that which the Church eventually came to call its faith arose in its life of prayer and worship. The God *of* whom we speak is first of all the God *to* whom we speak and the God *with* whom we think his thoughts after him. In prayer we learn a way of perceiving and thinking about life in God's world. The norm of prayer is the norm of faith. Tertullian referred to the Lord's Prayer as a compendium of the Gospel.[1] David Willis of Princeton contends that the "Lord's Prayer is faith in the mother tongue," and further, that we "know by the company that keeps us."[2] This company gives us its way of talking to, with, and about God in his world. When one prays the Lord's Prayer one is *confessing* a theology and *committing* oneself to the implications of the prayer. Let it then be true: to pray is to confess, to confess is to pray; to pray and confess is to commit one's life to the vocation of being a "little Christ." To pray Jesus' prayer commits one to him and to his faith.

Even if such be only partially the case, we in the Protestant tradition may want to give more than a patronizing nod to Ignatius's idea of "thinking with the Church." If God is our Father then the Church must be our mother. From Augustine to Calvin there was universal appreciation for the phrase, "Mother Church." The reason was that mothers not only give birth, they train their children. Parents are the primary company that "keep the children." "Mother Church" keeps her children by giving the language with which to think God's thoughts after him.

The most awesome thing parents do is give a language to their children, a point that will be developed in a later chapter. What makes it awesome is that the giving of language is a two-edged phenomenon. *Language limits.* It has the particularities of a given time, place, and culture. Communication often requires translation, and that at two levels. On the one hand, the most obvious translation takes place between two different language systems. On the other hand, even persons speaking the same language require "translation," because perceptions of meaning vary and personal inhibitions keep us from saying what we want to say. The helping professions, many of which are translators, "help us say it"—pastoral counselors, social workers, psychiatrists, and so on.

But a more basic limitation is that we are hearers before we are speakers. We learn to speak by repeating what we hear. The ear is the source of speech and therefore a teacher of the tongue. Moreover, the ear is fully formed by the seventh month of pregnancy so that when we are born, our ears are fully developed.[3] Unlike the eyes, the ears never close. What this amounts to is a fundamentally open character in all human beings. In this we are like God, in whose image we have been made, and whose ears are never shut. God is always open to our cries. When we close our ears, we are unlike God and we are inhuman. When the ears are closed we can no longer respond because the source of need is unrecognized. Human beings are fundamentally responding beings. We are first hearers, then speakers. Isaiah writes, "Who is blind but my servant, or deaf as my messenger whom I send? Who is blind as my dedicated one, or blind as the servant of the Lord? He sees many things, but does not observe them; his ears are open, but he does not hear" (Isaiah 42:19,20). Careful listening increases our capacity to be helpful to others. It also contributes to the liberation that language offers.

*Language liberates.* It is certainly a major vehicle of self-transcendence. The process of self-understanding is made possible by language. Here language is also an instrument of freedom and self-expression, both major components of the "coming into being" of a person. Think of the power present when a child says, "ball." An object has a name. It is known. Then think of what happens when a child says, "*my* ball." The child is beginning to identify what is his or hers. Then comes knowing what is yours and what is not yours. With language, the world gets ordered. There are family and friends, which are two different realities. There are friends and enemies, another set of realities. Language is part of the way we know the world and our relation to it. Words indicate ways of relating to the world. Words become ways of life. The norm of conversation—how we name things—becomes the norm for the course of life. Mother Church and mothers in general give words and, with them, a way of life. With this awareness it is much easier to understand the formula with which this chapter started: the norm of prayer became the norm of believing. By teaching us how to pray and in part *what* to pray, Mother Church was giving us a way of looking at the world. With the words comes a way of life. The ear was teaching the tongue.

Language is an awesome power precisely because, as Robert Jenson has noted, it has "metalinguistic"[4] qualities. The word means "after or beyond the words." Words and conversation have after effects, which are often more powerful than the words spoken. Thus meaning exceeds the definition of words found in the dictionary; it also sets a direction. As we have already pointed out, the norm of conversation is the norm of the course of life. Mother Church has given us a language that is also metalinguistic. Doctrine and direction are wedded in the theological language of prayer and worship.

That is what initially struck me about the Lord's Prayer. Jesus taught us more than how to pray; he taught us *what* to pray and laid the foundation for the notion that what is prayed is what is believed and what is believed is prayed. What is both prayed and believed is to become the dominant concern of the life of the pray-er. As Heschel so correctly said, in prayer we are to get to the place where felt human need begins to coincide with God's ends.[5]

The very language of the Lord's Prayer gives us concepts and forms a consciousness. Take one example from the prayer. God is named and praised as Father. What does this mean?

Normally, when we call somebody a father we imply that he has a wife and children. Father thus means more than an individual. It is a relational term. If there are several children in a family, when any one of them says "Father," they are, with the saying of that word, implying a relation among themselves through their parents. To call him "Father" is to say simultaneously, "brother and sister." A consciousness of family relations begins to emerge with the concept, father.

Jesus taught us to say, "Our Father. . . ." The address is plural—"Our." Those who use the plural pronoun are doing exactly what goes on in a family: when we call God by that term we are implying a set of relations on our part. In the family of God we are brothers and sisters to all who belong to God. In this specifically Christian use of the word, we are God's children by adoption (Galatians 4:5). To say, "Father" is at the same time to say "brother and sister."

But is that all? I think not. There is more here than just a consciousness of fellow Christians. In Acts 17:29, Paul speaks of all people as "God's offspring." Daring word! Offspring. Is it not the case that when we call God "Father," we imply a relation of brother and sister to every human being? God is our common source. When we say brother or sister to anyone we are acknowledging this source and acknowledging our obligation to the entire human family. To name God as Father is simultaneously to name others as family members.

Just this one example from the Lord's Prayer shows what it means to acknowledge that the norm of praying is the norm of believing. We confess what we pray. We make commitments to that for which we pray. In the process of praying a consciousness is formed. We not only pray for the Church; we pray with the Church.

A notation belongs here. By retaining the biblical language for God, it would be an oversimplification to assume an exclusively masculine meaning. Biblical narrative will not permit it. In the Song of Moses, God is celebrated as the Rock that bore Israel and the One who gave them birth (Deuteronomy 32:18). The blessings of the Messianic age are compared to "consoling breasts" (Isaiah 66:11), Jerusalem is likened to a mother (Isaiah 66:13), and, finally, God comforts his people as does a mother (Isaiah 66:13). And perhaps the crowning text is this: " 'Can a woman forget her sucking child, that she should have no compassion on the son of her womb?' Even these may forget, yet I will not forget you" (Isaiah 49:15).

Jesus likened himself to a hen (Matthew 23:37). In the parable in Luke 15:8-10, God is compared to a woman seeking a lost and badly needed coin. Continuing in the New Testament, Paul likened himself to a nurse (1 Thessalonians 2:7) and spoke of himself as being in travail for the Galatians until Christ was formed in them (Galatians 4:19).

In the case of the prayer that Jesus taught us, the Bible must inform our understanding of God. God seeks no "macho" image. What God is cannot be encompassed in a sexist category. Being maternal is not foreign to God.[6]

By means of the given language and forms of worship we are caught up into a Christological mystery: we pray with Christ to the same Father and in so doing the concerns of God which became the concerns of Christ now become our concerns. The preoccupation of both Christ and ourselves is God and his will. The Lord's Prayer and the Lord's life coincided, as did his needs and God's ends. The agenda of the Lord's Prayer was the agenda of his life. What he prayed he confessed; what he confessed he prayed; what he prayed and confessed coincided in his life. Jesus not only prayed what he lived; he lived what he prayed. The norm of conversation between him and God became the norm of the course of his life. To give a language is to grant the condition, both for conversation and the course of life.

This line of development can now take another step. Mother Church has not only given us the language of prayer but also that theology by means of the liturgy. The recent work of Gerard Lukken has begun to show how Roman Catholic theology, especially since Vatican Council II, has renewed its interest in the distinction between *theologia prima* (primary theology as prayer, praise, and liturgy) and *theologia secunda* (secondary theology as teaching and reflection). As he says:

> *The phrases* theologia *and* orthodoxia prima *then point to the liturgy in which faith is expressed and as such the liturgy is the first source and norm from which teaching is derived. Faith is expressed in the most original, reliable, and compelling way in the liturgy. God gives himself completely to man and man abandons himself to God in Jesus and through the Holy Spirit in the liturgical complex of words and symbols.*[7]

The liturgy tells a story. It uses the Christian year to show how God entered our history. The story involves a person, Jesus of Nazareth, and his life and work. By hymns, creeds, Scripture, sacraments, and prayer his life and work are commemorated, celebrated, and confessed. The story is kept alive by its retelling. Every year we repeat it and retell it. As Lukken said, it is by this annual and weekly retelling that we abandon ourselves to God in Christ by the power of the Holy Spirit. We tell the story to get a story, a story that addresses me in my need so that my story can be taken up in the larger story of God in Christ.[8] The story—sung, spoken, and acted out in liturgy—is the point of entry.

Read Deuteronomy 26:5-11. Each year as the Hebrew farmer brought the first of his harvest to the tabernacle for the support of its ministry and to offer thanks to God for the harvest, he repeated these words. Note that it is the story of the descent into Egypt and the exodus of his people. In God's deliverance of the former generation lay the farmer's own deliverance. He became part of this story by retelling it, for in retelling it he was confessing and claiming God as his own. His own story is taken up into a larger story and thus he finds himself in the exodus. He abandons himself to the future of this same God.

For us, the Apostles' Creed is much the same. So is the ancient hymn, the "Te Deum" (*The Covenant Hymnal,* 1973, No. 796). Note that their structure is just like Deuteronomy 26:5-11. All three have story lines. By confessing the Christian statements we claim Christ as our story so that, being in Christ, we are also in his resurrection, our exodus from death. From these we derive our consciousness as a people. By this language we name our God, his work, his promises, and his grace.

Mother Church, by teaching us what to pray, has taught us who we are and what we can expect. As the early Pietists would say, she has answered our three fundamental questions:

1. What am I to know?
2. What am I to do?
3. What am I to hope?

The words given in worship are a way *to* life and a way *of* life.

But let's ask how given language can also minister in a more personal way. How can it help me appropriate God's grace?

People who use regularly the *Book of Common Prayer* in worship hear this prayer annually on Ash Wednesday:

> *Almighty and everlasting God, you hate nothing you have made and forgive the sins of all who are penitent: Create and make in us new and contrite hearts, that we, worthily lamenting our sins and acknowledging our wretchedness, may obtain of you, the God of all mercy, perfect remission and forgiveness; through Jesus Christ our Lord, who lives and reigns with you and the Holy Spirit, one God, for ever and ever. Amen.*[9]

Think of the power and assurance in those words! God hates nothing he has made. By contrast, how often do we not hold in contempt what our hands have done or not done? We hate the work of our hands. God does not hate the work of his hands. We who are his workmanship are not objects of his disdain. He hates nothing he has made. We may think ourselves to be our own worst enemy. Do not project that image of yourself on God. Let your ear teach your tongue. Let your ear be open: God hates nothing he has made.

Or this prayer:

> *Almighty and everlasting God, you are always more ready to hear than we are to pray, and to give more than we either desire or deserve: Pour upon us the abundance of your mercy, forgiving us those things of which our conscience is afraid, and giving us those good things for which we are not worthy to ask, except through the merits and mediation of Jesus Christ our Savior; who lives and reigns with you and the Holy Spirit, one God, forever and ever. Amen.*[10]

Things of which our conscience is afraid! The list can get long. But before we become intimidated by the list, note that our conscience is to take courage because of God's mercy toward us *already*. We have confidence before God because he extends himself to us as we are. God is greater than our hearts (1 John 3:19,20). Before we are asked to do anything, it is announced to us that God has had mercy on us. Let the ear teach the tongue.

These two examples of how Mother Church gives us language only verifies Lukken's point. It is in the givenness of the liturgy and the words in worship that we can abandon ourselves to God in Christ by the power of the Holy Spirit. The words *first* acclaim God's work for us, i.e., the basis of the petition. The words help us enter the story of Jesus and his life and work for us. With the words comes the way. First we hear, then we respond. The words begin to form not only concepts of God but a consciousness that God is "for me" no matter what. This word from God keeps us alive in Christ and alert to life.

So we reaffirm: the law of prayer is the law of faith; what is prayed is confessed; what is confessed is prayed. Mother Church has given us a language that is the heart and mind of the spiritual life.

If the Lord's Prayer supplies a language framework for spirituality, Christology—the doctrine of Christ's life and work —supplies the lifestyle. Liturgical language, as Lukken noted, supplies a helpful way of thinking about Christ's life and work. The liturgical churches are particularly alert to the phrase, "paschal mystery." The focus is on the living of Christ's redeeming vocation, particularly as it centers on the *representative* notion present in the incarnation and on the *sacrificial* notion present in the atonement. Liturgy is a form of summarizing and remembering the mode of our salvation—Christ's incarnation, atonement, exaltation, and promised return. The liturgy does not only instruct us; it envelopes us in the paschal mystery. Liturgy as prayed doctrine, using the Christological language concerning Jesus' person and work, can provide us a spirituality that recapitulates in our lives the mystery which is Jesus Christ. What does this mean?

The word "recapitulate" means "to summarize." When a story is summarized it is "gone over again" or "redone." It happens again in the summary. As I am using the term, then, a spiritual person is a summary of Christ's life and work. In a certain sense, Christ is done over again in one's life. This is the specifically Christian use of the term "spiritual."

But what exactly is done over? The mystery of dying in order to live is at the heart of it. Robert J. Cronin found that out. The more he gave of himself, the more there was to give. In order to give himself to those boys the usual signs of security had to be given up. Yet the more insecure he became in the usual sense, the more secure he became in a sense of justice and truth. Truth makes people free. The mystery in all of this is that such effort has to wait for its vindication just as Jesus had to wait for his resurrection. Yet God's vindication is never to be known apart from the risk of faith and faithfulness. This is known only in obedience. It is hardly ever known as mere information. The mystery is that in dying we live. In our dying we are made alive. This is what I am after in spirituality—a redoing of the mystery of Christ's death and resurrection in the living of daily life. This is the paschal mystery, the Easter mystery.

Since Christian spirituality as I use the term connotes a "redoing" of the Christ-event in the lives of Christians, I will use the appropriate expressions. They are: active and passive obedience, representation and substitution, and the prophet-priest-king motif, already used in the Cronin story.

It is one thing to do Christological thinking. It is quite another thing to think Christologically. In the case of the former, "Christological" is an adjective modifying "thinking" in which case it denotes thinking about a specific subject-matter: Christology. Christology concerns itself with the intellectual and dogmatic issues regarding the person and work of Christ. For example, why Christ is confessed as having two equal natures: divine and human. The meaning and defense of that concept is the subject-matter of Christology.

But what might it mean to think Christologically? This adverbial use connotes a qualitative dimension within the thinking process itself. It denotes no subject-matter. More descriptive than definitive, more directional than discursive, to think Christologically is not to think out a position at all. When one thinks Christologically one does not arrive at any sort of conclusion. One does not resolve an intellectual problem and then dismiss the issue to the oblivion of worked-out issues, thus providing more archeological material for Ph.D. students!

Instead, to think Christologically means that one is initiated, not into a *query* for answer to the question, "Who is Jesus Christ and how is he constituted?" but rather into a *quest* for one's *relationship to the world as Christ*. To think Christologically is to think vocationally of oneself as a "little Christ." To be visionary in this Christologically qualified sense is to "see" all of existence in its relation to Christ and to see Christ in relation to all of existence. One "thinks" from within one's position in Christ, with Christ, for Christ, and through Christ. But how is such a vocation best described?

I find it helpful to utilize some concepts that were dominant in Reformation theologies. If one consults the compendia of theology compiled in the Lutheran instance by Heinrich Schmid and in the Reformed instance by Heinrich Heppe one finds an exceedingly precise and protracted discussion of the active and passive obedience of Jesus Christ. After distinguishing between the ministry of satisfaction and intercession, one finds this definition of obedience under the heading of satisfaction in Heppe:

> *The satisfaction rests entirely upon the voluntary obedience with which Christ gave himself up for the world, by his subjecting himself on the one hand to the will or* mandatum *(mandate or command) of the Father for the elects' sake and on the other hand to punishment for the transgression of the law for them also, i.e., by his complete fulfillment of the law (his* obedentia activa *or active obedience); and his bearing on the cross the full punishment for the transgression of the law (his* obedientia passiva *or passive obedience).*[11]

Jesus' obedience in life as well as in death commits the fulness of his person toward the redemption of humanity, treating no person or encounter as incidental to redemption but as integral to it. What Jesus *undertook* (his active obedience) is as significant as what he *underwent* (his passive obedience).

Within this framework one can "think Christologically," because the categories of active and passive obedience are integral to the Christian life. The Christian does in fact confront the living of life at two levels: what is *undertaken* and what is *undergone*. Indeed, what one has undertaken, either as a priestly or prophetic act, may require one to undergo a "testing as though by fire."

Recall now the story of R.J. Cronin in which there is both an active and passive obedience. Active because Cronin fulfilled the law, i.e., "You shall love your neighbor as yourself." He became the neighbor à la the story of the good Samaritan. This is what he *undertook*. Passive obedience is present in that he *underwent* not just the normal frustration that accompanies such altruistic intentions, but because in the cross-burning incident he found himself "open and bare" before the entire neighborhood. In point of perception, if not in fact, he was now at one with and a part of the very persons resented by his neighbors. He had both *identified with* and become *representative of* those disenfranchised people. Identification and representation are both Christologically useful terms. Cronin suffered, "the just for the unjust," that a quality of healing and hope might be made present and effective. He was both humble and humiliated. He knows what it meant to call God "Father."

The spirituality of which I speak finds the categories of active and passive obedience congenial because they conform to Christ's mode of being *in* the world and his mode of being *for* the world. The form is a given: Jesus Christ. The prayer he taught us was the agenda for his existence. Because we are his and have been inserted by faith and baptism into the paschal mystery, his agenda is ours. Jesus Christ is both our Lord and our life.

It is our agenda to recapitulate in our lives the *language about* and the *life of* Jesus of Nazareth. When we do so it will be evident that we are alive in Christ and alert to life.

## ENDNOTES

1. Tertullian, "On Prayer" in *The Ante-Nicene Fathers,* eds. Alexander Roberts and James Donaldson and enlarged by A. Cleveland Coke (Grand Rapids: William B. Eerdmans Publishing Co., Reprint 1980), p. 681.
2. David Willis, *Daring Prayer* (Atlanta: John Knox Press, 1977), pp. 48, and 36.
3. Charles Cummings, *The Mystery of the Ordinary* (San Francisco, et al.: Harper and Row, 1982), chapter 1.

4. Eric W. Gritsch and Robert W. Jenson, *Lutheranism* (Philadelphia: Fortress Press, 1976), pp. 42-44.

5. Abraham Joshua Heschel, *The Prophets* (New York and Evanston: Harper and Row, 1962), p. 190.

6. See Paul King Jewett, *The Ordination of Women* (Grand Rapids: William B. Eerdmans Publishing Company, 1980), pp. 35-47. See also *Language and the Church,* ed. Barbara A. Withers (Division of Education and Ministry, National Council of Churches in the U.S.A., 1984) for a collection of articles pro and con on the inclusive language question.

7. Gerard Lukken, "The Unique Expression of Faith in the Liturgy," tr. David Smith, *Concilium,* ed. Herman Schmidt and David Power (New York: Herder and Herder, 1973), pp. 19-20.

8. With regard to the meaning of stories I have been helped by Steven Crites, "The Narrative Quality of Experience," *Journal of the American Academy of Religion* XXXIX (September, 1971); Crites, "Angels We Have Heard" in *Religion as Story,* ed. James B. Wiggins (New York et al.: Harper Forum Books, 1975); Charles Winquist, *Practical Hermeneutics* (Chico, CA: Scholars Press, 1980); and Henri Nouwen, *The Living Reminder* (New York: The Seabury Press, 1977).

9. *Book of Common Prayer* (New York: The Seabury Press, 1977), p. 217: Collect for Ash Wednesday.

10. Ibid., p. 234: Proper 22.

11. Heinrich Heppe, *Reformed Dogmatics,* tr. G.T. Thompson, rev. and ed. Ernst Bizer and with Foreword by Karl Barth (Grand Rapids: Baker Book House, Reprint, 1978), pp. 458ff.

# CHAPTER 7

# *The Word Beyond the Words*

*T*he previous chapter advanced the idea that the norm of praying was the norm of believing. "Mother Church" gave language to her children. This language, derived from Scripture and worship, shaped the Christian's view of life and the world. The language given included a life-style and a thinking-style that lives according to God's truth and thinks God's thoughts after him. The point is, the language is given to us. Put another way, as the previous chapter also indicated, we know by the language that keeps us. When we are given words, we are given a way of life.

It is the purpose of this chapter to adapt the formula, "The norm of prayer is the norm of faith," to "The norm of communication is the norm of the course of life." This chapter will also make use of the formula, "We know by the language that keeps us." The communication of parents to children especially is the crucial element in the child's view of him- or herself and in the way the child develops relations to others. Alertness to this issue is fundamental to the spiritual formation of the person.

Communication is more than words. It includes words but it is more. Effective communication requires more than the advice,

"Keep talking." Talking helps. Talking can also hinder communication, especially when a "wordy" person drowns the other in a flood of language in order to avoid the real issue or to forestall a confrontation with the truth. But the fact remains, talking is a key element, as this poem "Keep Talking," written by a student at Southern Illinois University, shows:

> *All problems are not merely verbal,*
> *The philosopher tells me in uncounted thousands of*
> *    words—but*
> *I tried making love with my mouth taped shut*
> *    and I lost my love.*
> *I tried making friends with my mouth taped shut*
> *    and I lost my friend.*
> *I tried making war with my mouth taped shut*
> *    but no one was angry and the shouting stopped.*
> *I went about the street with my mouth taped shut*
> *    and they took me to the nuthouse.*
> *Where I am to this day,*
> *    wondering*
> *If all problems are not merely verbal.*

Language has its limitations. Communication between persons is limited if a German is attempting to speak with an American and neither knows the other's language. Communication is also limited when one wants to convey a profound feeling or impression to another. Then words are not enough. The matter is not merely verbal. Nor is it sufficient to say, "Keep talking." Words run out or do not go deep enough. Other "language" is called for—like a hug or an intense look into each other's eyes. The limitation factor in language is also known by those who have sought therapy for purposes of psychological self-understanding. As one draws nearer to the problem, words get scarce and seem insufficient. The therapist may then ask, "You mean. . . ?" Or the therapist may ask, "Is it like. . . ?" In all of these instances more is being communicated than a sentence. A self is trying to get communicated or given to the other. The whole matter of communication is more than "merely" verbal. The advice, "Keep talking," while helpful, is not the whole matter.

Even the matter of talking is more than "merely" verbal. Let us take the example of parents teaching their children how to speak. Part of this process is teaching them how to form their lips, position the tongue, and practice pronouncing words. That alone takes great effort and patience on the part of the parent. On the part of the child it takes practice and persistence. But that alone is not the whole story about teaching children how to speak.

Parents give their children language. The ear teaches the tongue. They are not born with a ready-made vocabulary. It is a parental privilege to give that to children. But even that is more than "merely" verbal. It is a fundamental error to overlook the spiritual character of teaching people how to talk. Talking involves naming, giving labels, identifying and classifying people, places, and things. It does not appear to be a very momentous matter to tell one's child that a thing with four legs and a flat top or some resemblance thereof is a "table" in English or *Tisch* in German. And so the vocabulary grows: "This is a brick," "That is a car," "That is a cow."

But all things change when we introduce children to other kinds of naming. "He is a 'nigger.' " "They are from the other side of the tracks." "I'm gonna 'Jew' him down." Because the Native Americans live more by the rhythms of nature than by the clock, I have heard it said "Indians are lazy." One can almost see and hear racial slurs and ethnic stereotypes and anti-Semitism. The visual and vocal aspects of these expressions acquire a vitality beyond measure. As the previous chapter noted, these expressions are metalinguistic. The after-effects linger after the sounds of the words die out. These are more or less *intentional* examples. What they show is that naming involves valuing. In teaching children how to speak we communicate along with it a value system. The norm of conversation will become the norm of the course of life because we know by the language that keeps us.

What perhaps may be an even more profound and pervasive aspect of communication is how children are taught to speak *unintentionally.* Let us suppose that someone lives in an area of tension between ethnic groups. Frequently in such areas one group does not understand the history and culture of the other. As a matter of fact, seldom does one have friends except within one's own group. So the isolation of people from each other creates a climate for intimidation. Then some incident occurs involving one of the ethnic groups and a father blurts out, "Those goddamn so-and-so's!" These kinds of expressions are often heard watching the evening news when something offending our prejudices or convictions is seen. Then father's commentary in the form of profanity or slang drives it home. It is an unforgettable event for a child.

This is an event. It is a communication-event. More than sentences are involved. This is actually a formation process. The heart and the mind—the very being of the child is being determined. When one gives language to children, intentional or unintentional, one begins to limit freedom and to direct their lives. Words, put together in sentences and spoken in a given context, are determinative, in part at least, of the child's mode of relating to others. Communication, as found in the above context, commits a child to a direction. When children are taught how to speak, they are being told how things are to be named. To name is to establish a relation between you and what is named. Naming brings the relation into being. Anything that involves relations is inherently spiritual. Naming is one of the highest privileges given to humankind. It is also the profoundest responsibility. God left the entire naming process to Adam at creation. Free to name! Free to damn! Free to value! "What's in a name?" Most everything.

But I want to return to the theme of the communication event. When a child hears profanity used in naming someone a "goddamn so-and-so," more is communicated than words. When such powerful language is used, a child *hears* not only the words but a tone of voice; he or she also *sees* the facial expression accompanying the tone. One sees as well as hears the naming process. My recollection of a piece of psychological research may help reinforce this point. Some argue that sight is the chief objectification of consciousness. Who can measure the terror of *seeing* someone swear in hatred or in a seizure of prejudice? The impression made on a young person must go very deep. This communication event then gets both complex and subtle. It is complex because it involves words, tone, and facial expression. It is subtle because the sight of the face and the memory of tone get associated with certain peoples and/or situations and a relationship therewith is instituted. Language and destiny get intertwined—all very real but hardly noticed at the time. I agree with Amos Wilder: "The language of a people is its fate."[1] A conversation, a communication-event has become the norm of the course of life.

In this communication-event it is also to be noticed that one has not fully understood the event if one thinks that one can get the meaning of a sentence just by knowing the definition of the words. One can look up the words "God" and "damn" and get a good idea of the thought of the person speaking. But if facial expression and tone of voice belong to this subtle and complex situation, then definition of words is but one-third of the communication-event. Two-thirds of the meaning of the event lies outside what can be found in the dictionary. Definition and meaning are related but they are not identical. The communication-event, then, does more than convey ideas, propositions, facts, and information. This event actually exercises a certain control over the other, but especially the children. Language does involve definition of terms. It also directs a life. Language in particular and the communication-event as a whole are nothing other than either spiritual formation or spiritual deformation. And all because it concerns the power to name—which is also the power to bless or to curse, to heal or destroy, to kill or to make alive.

Earlier in this chapter it was noted that communication by language reaches its limit. Then other means of communication are employed. The use of the body is present in all communication, as for example in the use of gestures—or even more fundamentally, the use of the mouth and ears. Communication requires the means by which what needs to get to the other person can in fact get there. This requires material beyond the body. Take sound, for example. It makes vibrations in the ear by the use of the material components that cause and constitute the vibrations. It can hardly be argued, then, that communication can be carried out in the fullest sense of the term without materials and without means. These complex and subtle components make the act of communication an event carried out at more than one level of human understanding. In this event of communication, *impressions* are made as well as *information* conveyed. Sometimes the impressions (tone of voice and facial expression) are more powerful than the information—more memorable, too, and hence at times even more foundational. Sign and symbol accompany words in almost every act of communication.

In the Christian Church this fact has been accounted for in the language and practice of administering and receiving the sacraments of Holy Baptism and Holy Communion. It has already been noted that communication in any ordinary human situation uses both words and acts (gestures, facial expression, etc.). Both are required in order to communicate the "self" and what the "self" intends to say. The signs and symbols help the "self" to give itself away and in turn be received, interpreted, and known by another. Self-giving is part of communication.

Augustine took note of this factor and has helped the Church understand the mystery of the sacraments by understanding the mystery of communication. It involves both words *and* signs. He noted, for example, that a word comes to an element and so there is sort of a "visible word." But note, it is a combination of word and element. He also observed that at times elements impress themselves on the senses and, by means of that, one has a knowledge of something more than just the element which is being felt or tasted or seen or smelled. Now that is a bit theoretical so let us analyze it by taking an example from everyday life.

Suppose that your son or daughter has been driving for a relatively short period of time. While driving one evening, he or she has a slight accident. You the parent help care for the details that need to be carried out: police report, insurance forms, and so forth. You also, of course, try to understand and relate to the many feelings your son or daughter has, to say nothing of your own. Then suppose that on another occasion, not too long after the first accident, he or she has an accident with the other car. You the parent are sitting in the living room in the later part of the evening when your child comes home. You know by the walk— by the way your son or daughter carries his or her body—and by the facial expression that something is wrong. You know it because of body language, even though a word hasn't been spoken. You have an impression and the impression is so real, so clear, that it is almost a kind of information: yet no facts have been shared. The child slowly sits down in a chair at some distance from you and is silent. After a bit you may say something like, "Is something wrong?" Or, "Is there anything you want to tell me?" The child says, "I'm gonna quit driving." You ask, "Why?" The response comes back, "I had another accident." After some time goes by, during the course of which you get the facts in order and gather what information is needed, you know your parental care is not done.

Now comes the key moment in this incident. You can stay seated in your chair and try to encourage your child. You can speak words of affirmation across the distance between the two chairs. It may be nice for your child to hear it but I doubt that it makes much of an impression. The words are more dead than alive. But you have another choice. You can get up from your chair and go over to your child and embrace him or her *while you speak.* Now you have made an impression and have reached more deeply into your child's being than the brain. This is being more than "merely" verbal. While you are speaking words of understanding and affirmation, or perhaps even sharing a similar event with your child from your youth, you are *giving yourself* to your child by means of an embrace and at the same time you are receiving your child into your acceptance. Grace gets communicated by gestures. Gestures make it possible to participate in an event of grace. Of course, gestures can also exclude from grace.

Let us return to Augustine. He had noted that an element impresses itself on the senses, but that in addition to having knowledge of the element, one has knowledge of more than the element. With the element came the knowledge of something beyond it. Now in the case of my example, the element is the embrace. The child *feels* the embrace and *hears* the words. Along with the embrace, which is felt, and the words, which are heard, the child has knowledge of acceptance, of still being in the good graces of Dad or Mom. The communication is not from a distance. It is by identification of the parent with the child. A word has accompanied the element and so there is a visible, an audible, and an impressionable word. I have an idea that at the time, the signs of acceptance are more powerful than spoken words. This communication event conveys a knowledge beyond words, but it could not be complete without the words. In, with, and under the element there is conveyed a lively and powerful reality.

But this process also works negatively. I read of a Ku Klux Klan rally when the evening ended in the cross-burning ritual. Earlier there had been harangues about Blacks, filled with innuendo and explicit intimidation. Children of the Klan members were also present, since what better educational setting can one find for the communication of such matters than language and ritual where the body gets into the act and the senses find full participation? Just think of it: the sight of numerous crosses in flames; the sound of chants; the smell of burning wood—it could not be a more wholistic event involving nearly all of the senses. Talk about elements impressing themselves on the senses, conveying a knowledge beyond themselves! But then comes the clincher. According to the report of this rally, the reporter spoke of a Klansman picking up his child as the crosses burned and saying something to this effect as he made sure the child gazed at the light of the fire: "Look honey, take a good look; it's white." All the while he was speaking he hugged the child in the most paternal way possible. Words and elements, speech and sign/symbol—all communication is sacramental from the beginning. By the way, need I ask what color the burned crosses were? He got this point across, vocally and visually. Make no mistake about it. The little children at this event learned by the language that kept them and the norm of conversation became the norm for a course of life. With words comes a way of life.

Positively or negatively, no symbols, no communication. A word beyond the words is required. Audible words require visible words.

God uses the two ways to get to us as well: word and symbol. He also puts words and elements together. He gives us audible words and visible words. At Holy Communion, for example, as you *see* the bread, *feel* it, and *taste* it, maybe even *smell* it, you hear: "This is my body which is for you. Do this in remembrance of me." Notice the words: ". . . my body . . . for you." The point is that someone is for us now. This "someone" is Jesus of Nazareth, the one in whom dwelt all the fulness of the

Godhead bodily. God—for us, in the flesh, in communion with us. If God is for us who can be against us?

Just as Jesus established real, tangible relations with people who had no idea that he would even darken the doors of their homes, so he has commanded this meal with him. It is not in memory of him. That would be of little value, for it would be in memory of an absence. The meal is in fellowship with him and with all others who are in him. He comes to us, desires to eat with us, to give himself *to* us, and to be there *for* us. Hence our tradition has spoken of his real presence, for it is on him that we depend for acceptance, for being able to see ourselves as he sees us. To be seen as he sees us opens up a new perspective on us and on each other. Faith lets the bread be what he said it was: "my body, which is for you." Body means presence, availability, and accessibility.

In this fashion God not only communicates about himself to us. He gives himself.

As Augustine said, with the element comes a knowledge of something other than the element. With a hug to a distraught child comes a knowledge of something other than the touch of flesh and a rise in body heat. When God uses word and symbol, a communication-event is occasioned just as when a parent's word of affirmation is accompanied by a hug. In this case the word "symbol" does not refer to a picture or image that points away from itself to another. The way I am using the word "symbol" does not just mean that it "reminds" me of someone. As I have used the word "symbol," it refers to a communication-event in which the symbol conveys in part what it signifies. It is more than a pointer or illustration. The symbol is part of the reality being given and is therefore essential to the communication process.

The hug does more than just point to a parent's intention. The hug is the communication of the parent's desire to be accepting of the child and it overcomes the distance between a child who feels distant and fearful and a parent who hold a massive amount of authority over the child. The words and hug communicate what they signify: acceptance and understanding.

The sacraments of Christ's institution are communication-events. They do not just point away to him. Because his Word accompanies the bread which is the vehicle of his presence for us, we are caught up into Christ's fellowship. He, like the parent, initiates the process by extending word and symbol, making them the means of his grace. I would find it next to impossible to live without the twofold ministry of Christ's to us: word and sacrament.

ENDNOTES

1. Amos N. Wilder, *The Language of the Gospel* (New York: Harper and Row, 1964), p. 13.

# CHAPTER 8

# *In Search of Words*

*I*n the previous chapters we have noted how words bring a world view to expression. The language that keeps us helps us name the world and thus relate to it. In this chapter attention is focused on language and on bringing oneself to expression. By the way we name ourselves we relate to ourselves and God.

In Isaiah 50:4,5, the prophet says, "The Lord God has given me the tongue of those who are taught, that I may know how to sustain with a word him that is weary. Morning by morning he wakens, he wakens my ear to hear as those who are taught. The Lord has opened my ear, and I was not rebellious, I turned not backward." Three things stand out in this text. The first is the instruction of the tongue. It needs to be taught what to say and how to say it. Second, one of the reasons the tongue is taught is so that it might sustain others who are weary of life, who have no reason for hope, or those who have lost their way. Words are instruments of counsel and comfort. Such words are not spoken haphazardly. Appropriate words come from a tongue that has been taught. Finally there is the ear. One is to listen before one speaks. Nothing is worse than answering questions people are not asking. The ear is important for the instruction of the tongue. The ear helps the tongue take aim. What the tongue then says will not be idle words.

The search for words begins with oneself. In order to understand oneself one looks for a word that will help explore the meaning of an event or an experience. When such a word is found it most likely will not *explain* the experience but it will help *explore* the depth of the experience. Profound experiences are seldom explained. Part of the meaning of an explanation is that once one has accomplished it, nothing is left. The problem is solved and goes away. The experiences of life that are foundational and formative are not explained and do not go away. The more mature one becomes, the more one seeks to understand. Hence the preference for the term *explore* as opposed to the word *explain*.

One way of describing the situation may be as follows:

Life as it is lived involves three dimensions: ⎧heart
⎨head
⎩hands

I do not mean to divide the human personality into three separate and unrelated parts. These are dimensions of one reality— distinctions but not separations, as one of my teachers would phrase it. Modern medicine has made one more conscious than ever of the unity of the person. What happens in the body affects the spirit and the spirit in turn affects the body. So it is common to speak of "psychosomatic" illnesses—illnesses that derive from the influence of an anxious spirit on the physiology of the body. By the same token, a body that is in shape has an enormously positive influence on the spirit of the person.

But the diagram needs refining. By some expansion, it might look like this:

heart—impact—feeling
head—insight—thought
hand—involvement—doing

To begin with, the *heart* stands for that experience in life in which we are just impacted. The experience can be positive, like receiving an unexpected promotion, or negative, like living with or through a profound tragedy. At the time it hits, the experience has no meaning, sometimes even no name. We even use the impersonal pronoun "it." I have used the term "feeling." If the experience is positive, it may leave us speechless, breathless, or mystified. If is is negative, the experience leaves us at times stunned and feeling sick. All of this is impact, just raw impact. It awaits understanding.

That is where the head comes in. By its thought processes it seeks to give insight to whatever remains as raw impact. The head wants answers but does not always get them, especially when hard experiences stifle inquiry into their meaning. But we also have an urge that if we would explore the experience it just might be productive, to say nothing of healing. So the mind continues to nudge us ever closer to the all-important exploration. It wants insight. Our spiritual nature seeks satisfaction.

Finally, the hands are to be included in this process. They represent doing and involvement. It is entirely likely that if one begins to explore whatever has impacted one, one will find, sooner or later, a person who has had or is now in a similar experience. Your story may be just what is appropriate for that person's need for courage in order to begin to explore his or her own experience. But if each of us refuses to be truthful, to explore our own situations, we will be speechless in the presence of others. Remember Isaiah's word? We are to acquire tongues that have been taught so that we might sustain with words those who are weary One more thing: all of this requires good ears to make sure that we understand the other person properly. Then our tongue can be instructed by the question of the other as much as it has been previously instructed by what it has learned on its own.

Now an example. I once heard of a man and his wife to whom a profoundly deformed child had been born. Much surgery had been required. As I heard the story, the first question of the man was, "Why me?" Those two words were repeated for a long time. It was the only question. Then, a change came about. For some reason, as often happens, he was moved to ask another question—or maybe better, he was freed to see that he had not asked the only question. So he asked, "Why *not* me?" It is a profoundly different question. It represents a fundamental change in one's stance toward life, toward God, toward oneself, maybe even toward one's child. Anyway, this man was free to identify how limited his initial question had been.

But now I must add a qualifier. The first question was not wrong, sinful, or immoral. It is the first question. It is understandable. It is the way to *begin* to cope, to release feelings of anger, disappointment, and disillusionment—all of which need to be released. But as this person discovered, it was not the only question. By asking the new one, "Why not me?" the man discovered a new freedom to accept his child and himself.

Note the importance of language. It brought out into the open the honesty of the man, the recognition that other questions needed to be asked. If the only question is "Why me?" it is entirely possible to be so consumed by that question as to prevent one from relating constructively either to one's child or to one's wife. His tongue had begun the process of being taught. Insight was beginning to explore impact. The problem was being structured and understood—explored but not explained. The man discovered that once he had begun to address the issue, to name it, he could begin to talk with others in a similar circumstance. Once his tongue had begun to find words, it could share the words with others. Insights into an impact eventually led to involvement with others. The entire human being—heart, head, and hands—was now available to others for support and understanding. Because the questioner had been freed to ask a more personal and a more profound question—"Why *not* me?"—he was also freed the more to *receive* care as well as to give it. When the truth makes one free, one is free indeed—to listen to oneself and others and to speak to oneself and others. Then the tongue has been taught and the words are appropriate.

This same exploratory character of language can be found in the Bible. Paul describes his dramatic conversion experience in Acts 22:3-21 and 26:9-23. Much of the text is pure narration. At the end of the narrative in 22:21 the Lord tells Paul the he will be sent to the Gentiles. In 26:16 and following, Paul again recalls his commission to go to the Gentiles and preach to them the unsearchable riches of Christ. In the main, the passages recounted here from Acts describe the details of Paul's life as a persecutor of the Church and of his conversion. There is very little *reflection*.

But elsewhere in the writings of Paul the approach is different. Instead of *recounting* the story and narrating the sequence of the events of his life, these writings *reflect* on the story's meaning. They recount few, if any, details. In contrast, they explore the impact of this foundational event: a blasphemer and persecutor of the Church is made its foremost apostle to the Gentiles! By what stretch of the imagination can this be accounted for? An imagination—that's what it takes to even begin to come to terms with the impact of such a life-changing event. It defies explanation but invites exploration. That is exactly what Paul did: begin exploring this mystery of grace and mercy.

Recall the diagram:

> heart—impact—feelings
> head—insight—thought
> hand—involvement—doing

Paul sought a tongue that had been taught so that he might have words by which to understand his own experience of grace and, by doing so, encourage and instruct others.

So far as I can tell, there are at least five texts that reflect on the meaning of the Damascus road experience: 1 Timothy 1:12-17; 1 Corinthians 15:1-10; Philippians 3; 2 Corinthians 11:21ff.; and Galatians 1,2. I will look at two of these with the purpose in mind of noting how Paul uses language and metaphors or picture words to explore the impact of an unsearchable and inexhaustible expression of grace to him.

In 1 Timothy 1:12-17, Paul gives a personal testimony to Timothy. It would be interesting to know what evoked this testimony. What was it in Timothy's personal life or pastoral setting that required Paul to reach down into the depths of his own very painful and sordid past? In any case Paul tells him a story; he recounts his experience. In effect he tells Timothy that if he has reason to doubt his worthiness to be a pastor then he, Paul, has more. I repeat: in order for Paul to be of help, he must use a personal story. Timothy needs a witness, not an argument.

The text includes personal references to having been a persecutor and a blasphemer. It also includes Paul's self-understanding as having been the chief of sinners. At the same time, he is mystified at the sheer mercy of God shown to him—unanticipated, unexpected, and uninvited. Nevertheless, it is true: the Lord counted him worthy and appointed him a preacher of this good news.

But for Timothy, Paul reduces this entire event to one word: the reason the Lord did all this was to make him a pattern or example of his work of grace. It is almost like saying that Paul is a public advertisement of how God does things. As he said in another letter, "For we are his workmanship, created in Christ Jesus for good works" (Ephesians 2:10). To a young pastor, perhaps threatened by an awareness of some kind of spiritual inadequacy or memory of some disqualifying deed, Paul says in effect: "Take heart. If you think you have reason to renounce your call, I the more. But, Timothy, I am the pattern of God's work. I went from the foremost of sinners to the foremost of apostles. I, like you, am God's workmanship. The best we can do is to give ourselves to God to be his workshop. Then you will be a pattern of God's work for another." The words, "pattern" or "example" provide words for Paul to explore his experience and to express himself to another in need of self-understanding. Impact, insight, involvement.

But there is an even more expressive use of language in 1 Corinthians 15:1-10. The text is very familiar, since it is usually read each Easter. In the first part of the text Paul identifies the Christian message—Christ's death and resurrection. Then, as a kind of prologue to his own experience, he identifies those to whom the Lord has appeared (vv. 5-7). Finally, he gets autobiographical (vv. 8-10). He speaks of Christ's appearance to him as to one "untimely born." Other texts speak of this as an appearance to one "born out of due time." But the word as originally used, deriving from the medical profession, denotes a miscarriage or an abortion. It is a striking metaphor: a "miscarriage" or an "abortion" of an apostle. What does it possibly indicate?

Note first of all Paul's references to himself as the "least" of the apostles and his unfitness for apostolic work. The reasons for his unfitness? The same ones that shadow his letter to Timothy: his past life as a persecutor of the Church. Innocent people had fallen victim to him. But of all things, Paul is an apostle. Again, he is searching for a word by means of which he can gain insight into the impact made on him by the Damascus experience. Hence his use of a very perplexing metaphor: a miscar-riage of an apostle. What can such a painful word provide in terms of exploratory value?

I am impressed by the temporal character of the word. Both abortions and miscarriages are births before the time. They are premature in very radical ways. That perhaps was his clue. All births into the kingdom of God are births before the time. No one makes him- or herself fit and then asks God to accept him or her. Birth into God's grace comes ahead of time. That is its glory.

To be born again is to be untimely born,

> *Just as I am*
> *without one plea.*

That is the way it is. At the time of our new birth we may appear as having all the marks of sin—prejudice, remembered griev-ances, unresolved memories and relations, to say nothing of the record of spiteful deeds. Just as miscarriages and many an aborted birth have no beauty that we should want to behold them, so many converts newly born are nothing to behold behavior-wise. Precisely. They are untimely born. But born nevertheless! Premature to be sure, but prematurely *born* nevertheless.

> *Just as I am—*

That is where both God and we start the new life in Christ. And that is where God started with Paul. The word, negative in most contexts, was turned to positive use in order to under-stand the overwhelming experience of grace. When experience comes to language it can also come to expression. Or in Isaiah's word, Paul was acquiring a tongue that had been taught so that he could sustain with words those who were weary.

Notice now how my initial diagram has operated. Paul has had one fundamental experience of grace. To Timothy he used the word pattern—and, maybe by extension, the idea of an advertise-ment. People who are alive in Christ are walking billboards or advertisements of the power of grace to remake human life, to recreate the image of God. But to the Corinthians he had used the idea of premature birth to encapsule the work of the Gospel. In all of these texts he is speaking *to* himself and speaking *of* himself. Once more the diagram:

> heart—impact—feelings
> head—insight—thought
> hands—involvement—doing

It is by this means that Paul acquired a tongue that had been taught so that he could sustain with words—not only himself but others.

All Christians experience those times when God seems absent. Some speak of dry periods in the Christian life. How can one explore God's activity or lack of it in this dark time? How can one illumine one's own darkness? Is this painful for oneself only or does God have knowledge of what this means to the one enduring the dark night of soul?

Allow me an example from the mystical tradition. One of the Spanish mystics was enduring a long dark night of the soul. God seemed absent. The mystic wondered about the meaning of his loneliness and lostness. Why does God withdraw himself and draw his children into such darkness? The mystic was speechless—wordless for a time and therefore without a tool for exploring this experience. His tongue remained dumb.

Then, in the providence of God, he was struck by the powerful meaning in a very common sight in sixteenth-century Spain. Mothers nursed their children in public and at home. It was so ordinary. But then this common sight became insight. The mystic became aware of an extraordinary revelation. By being attentive to the mystery of nursing an infant, he received a new way to explore his own dark night of the soul.

Children who are nursed also have to be weaned. They must learn to drink from a cup and cope with learning the skills to do so. When it comes time to be weaned the child expresses frustration and fights to retain dependence on mother. Perhaps, then, as the weaning process goes on the child feels alienation and even some rejection. It is at any rate a complex and subtle event.

But mothers also have feelings. There is the breaking of the bonding process that has gone on. Bonding now must take place differently. She must relate to a person who will grow ever more independent. The weaning process is only the first event in a series of events—leaving for school, then for college, then for career, then for marriage, and on it goes. So the mother has her reluctances just as the child does. True, there is a joy in the anticipated freedom of less demanding bonding relations but there is also the sorrow of anticipating the final leaving. For mother as for child, weaning is both subtle and complex.

Now the mystic had possibly found a word. Weaning. He was being weaned from all false and immature dependence on God. God wanted him to grow up and grow into a living faith that could bear pain, endure crosses of all kinds, be steadfast in love and unswerving in hope. It was not exactly pleasurable for God to have to "push one into one's own" by withdrawing. But by doing so, God did force the mystic to ask questions and to inquire into the true state of his inner life. On the other hand, God could joyfully anticipate the freer and more personal faith of the one who had been weaned.

Having found a word, namely "weaning," this mystic now had a way to open the several facets of his experience of the dark night of the soul. Even though God had found it necessary to push him on to maturity, there was perhaps in God—as in mothers who wean their children—a pain, a wound of love. God is not untouched. With regard to himself, the mystic had noticed that the period of weaning is not forever. But while it lasts, he does not bear the pain alone. The one who weans does not escape either. There was now communion with God in the wound of love.

This process of weaning started as an impact on the heart. The meaning was not immediately apparent. But the mystic did not give up. Being alert to life he saw the weaning process as an insight, not an explanation. But with this insight comes reflection on life in general. It can lead to involvement.

There comes a time when parents have to let their children "learn for themselves." They "withdraw," they "wean" by letting children live with consequences of their own decisions. Parents cannot always intercept children on their way to foolish decisions. Some things are best learned by experience. True, weaning does not mean abandonment; parents are available. But it is unhealthy to prevent all mistakes.

In these situations, parents do find joy, even freedom, in

watching their children grow up. Satisfaction comes when their decisions show good judgment. But there is also pain when carelessness and irresponsibility force kids to endure unnecessary pain and embarrassment. Joy and pain go together in this process. But without weaning in some form, an unhealthy dependence can grow.

With a word one can unlock many levels of meaning. It does not explain pain. It does explore it and helps to understand it. By language we bring ourselves and our relations to self-expression and to prayer.

I will present two of my journal entries as an example of how I have used language to bring myself to expression and to prayer. This is one way I've acquired "a tongue that has been taught."

*September, 1976—Trinity Season*
*Now that I have been working on the problem of aging with my mother and father, aunt and uncle, I sense both the mercy and mercilessness of time.*

*Take mercilessness first. Now that only months exist until they move from Nebraska to Northbrook, time is inexorable in its process and inevitable in its outcome: they must leave a place where all have lived nearly fifty-three years, and where Dad and Joe have always lived. Uprooting is painful. You have to tell friends and then make new ones. Time is inevitably merciless. I learned that, too, when I left home for the first time to go away to school. The day came to end vacation and return again. On the day Mom and Dad and Frank left me about three on a Sunday afternoon for the first time when I began North Park studies, I remember how painful it was and how I fought tears from twelve to three as it dawned on me they were leaving.*

*So now they face it—mercilessly. Time calls us to new tasks, forces us to face an end of one sort or another.*

*But it's merciful too. Each time we have to tell someone—such as the folks have, too—the reality becomes more real, more actual, more faced. We inch our way into the reality or the reality impresses itself into our lives. But such is of mercy—that by the time, in this case, of change, change has been owned up to.*

*But also time is merciful in that after we pass through the inevitable, time moves us from as well as to that event. Distancing from is a healing, a coping. For just as reality is inexorably thrust upon us in repeated incidents prior to the inevitable, so reality is coped with after the inevitable. Distancing is a "grace-full" process. We can be thankful for the distancing, for up to the event is dread and after the event is distancing. Thank God.*

*August 1982—Pentecost/Trinity*
    *This has been a vexing summer. Mother and Dad have suffered pronounced decline in mind and body. I am in the process of having to move them to Brandel Care Center. Body functions are no longer under control. Dad is oblivious at times to who is there and what is going on. Mom forgets. She has no sense of time and can't hardly make the bed: she does not do the laundry.*
    *It is a strange spot to be in: to take over the destiny of two people whom you love very much. In some ways it seems to be a contradiction of love, i.e., love does not appear to want to take over the destiny of others. Macquarrie defines love as "letting be." This whole thing is a profound encounter with how love acts in an apparently contradictory way in order to remain love. If they were just "let be" it could be destructive to them, debilitating to their general health, and demeaning to their person. The senile easily become spectacles—how tragic. So love takes over and acts.*
    *That brings about a reversal. A son who is subject to parents and is to be submissive to their authority now becomes the one who exercises authority over them and takes over their destiny.*
    *It is a strange feeling to exercise authority, control, and destiny. Such power is dangerous because those over whom power is exercised are vulnerable and defenseless. They can get by on so little. Get by. That's a temptation—to cut corners on expenses for comforts and amenities. To cut corners on time—they don't really know. They are truly subject to me. But that term is not synonymous with subjugated. A person caring for elderly parents needs to know that and ever keep it in mind. Necessarily they are and must be subject but not subjugated. However weak, however fragile, however impotent, however unimpressive—no matter—they are subjects but are not to be subjugated. Even should they lose their mind totally, subject but not subjugated. A fine line. But necessary for their protection and mine.*

*All of this brings to mind Jesus' conversation with Peter dur-*
*ing Easter (John 21:18): "Truly, truly, I say to you, when you*
*were young, you girded yourself and walked where you would;*
*but when you are old, you will stretch out your hands, and*
*another will gird you and carry you where you do not wish to*
*go."*
*So true.*

I intend for these entries to stand as written and in their own
right. But do note how writing brings the self not only to
expression but also to examination. It was particularly helpful
to me to note a distinction in the August, 1982 entry between
my parents being *subject* to my care but not *subjugated*. It is a
fine line but it makes all the difference in the world. On the one
hand, it helped me to be free to act without guilt—though not
without regret. On the other hand, I was given proper limits
within which to act. I was not free to do as I please. Their per-
sonhood was my stewardship.

Thus I was helped to be alert to the fine line that distinguishes
issues. Yet learning about that line made me free to act. It has
also given me words to use with other people who face the
same problem. The heart, the head, and the hands now have
been brought into proper relation. Impact yielded to insight
and insight was translated into care for my parents and helpful
communication with others. The Christian sequence has been
followed in this threefold pattern of heart, head, and hand, for
the word is to become flesh.

# CHAPTER 9

# *Workers Together With Christ*

$T$he theme of prophetic or servant spirituality is taking on an assertive character in contemporary spiritual theology. To be sure, it has never been dead but it has often been dormant.

Like most disciplines, spiritual theology has also endured the threat of polarization. Liturgics has always steered a course between formalism and spontaneity. Systematic theology seems always to wonder what, if anything, Athens has to do with Jerusalem, or philosophy with theology. Practical theology is conscious of the fact that there is more to practicing a discipline than doing it.

Take counseling for example. Whose theories does one use? Freud's? Jung's? Mowrer's? How to do something is more than a question of technique. To practice a skill is to practice a theory. The crucial matter concerns what theory is chosen as a basis for one's work. Spiritual theology steers a course between those who describe it primarily as the contemplative life and those who describe it as a combination of the active and the contemplative life.

It is to the credit of Augustine that he referred to the spiritual life as a working combination of Mary and Martha. Serving in the name of Jesus was not inherently inimical to sitting at the feet of Jesus. The Mary and Martha combination is to be the course of the spiritual life. One example is John Woolman: Quaker, mystic, servant, and freedom fighter for the slaves. No one who reads his *Journal*[1] can get the notion that an active, serving life is inimical to the life of prayer and contemplation. Indeed, such concerns naturally flow out of a God-centered life.

One of the persistent tensions in the Christian life is between the life of prayer and the life of service. More technically, it is described as the relation between the active life and the contemplative life. Is it the case that the more withdrawn one is from the world, the better one can pray? Does life in the world—the ordinary world of business, parenting, education, farming, athletics, and so on—serve as a distraction to the life of prayer? Or does it in fact become the substance of the life of prayer—substance meaning adoration of God, thanksgiving for his blessings, confession of one's failures and sins, and intercession for needs that arise daily?

For some, the contemplative life, the life usually lived in some form of a Christian community, is a form of higher obedience, since one has left houses, lands, mothers, fathers, the possibility of marriage and promising career for the sake of Jesus Christ and his Gospel. At least that is the way this tradition understands Jesus' words to the rich young man in Matthew 19:16-22, especially verse 21. In order to be perfect, one must rid oneself of the encumbrances of the world to carry out perfect obedience to Christ. The monastic vows of poverty, chastity, and obedience stem from this tradition. But it is a tradition that places the stress on the contemplative life and, at the same time, would assert a very powerful kind of activity: the sacrifice of all worldly aspirations.

Augustine spoke of this tension as the struggle between Mary (the contemplative life) and Martha (the active life), based on the well-known text in Luke 10:38-42. Mary sits at Jesus' feet and listens to his word. Martha concerns herself with serving, with hosting this guest, with dinner and dishes. She even gets a bit annoyed with Mary, who seems not to have lifted a finger to help, which annoyance apparently makes Martha work more feverishly. Jesus calls this to Martha's attention and, at the same time, takes note of Mary's capacity for attentiveness to an appropriate moment. Mary had chosen the good part.

Perhaps the point here is that the possible annoyance felt so deeply by Martha rendered her incapable of attentiveness and awareness. Distracted by her annoyance at Mary, Martha was oblivious to the guest and maybe even to herself and to the forces that often work in the lives of activists. Activity by itself is not a virtue. It can be fueled by distraction as much as by dedication, by annoyance as much as by affection. Even dedication needs to be purified, lest what starts out as faithfulness ends up as fanaticism. The psalmist lamented that his zeal consumed him because of his foes (119:139). Paul expressed his concern about those who have zeal for God but not according to knowledge (Romans 10:2).

This seems to be a basic point between Jesus and Martha. Her annoyance at Mary fuels her activity and feeds her stress and if she is not careful she will be consumed by her own zealous activity. Annoyance can lead to animosity and anger and finally to alienation. But what is a warning *about* activism is not necessarily a put-down *of* it.

Mary's "good part"—her sitting at Jesus' feet and listening to his words, to say nothing of her attentiveness to him as a person—is not necessarily an elevation of the contemplative life to an exclusive position. There is a time for activity to cease and for attentiveness to become total. There is a time to stop, to listen, to be silent, to attend. The point needs emphasis: there is a time for undivided attentiveness to God's Word, to the inner self, and to others. Mary had chosen the "good part" because she had discerned the time to be quiet, to listen, to cease her ministry and to be ministered to. And perhaps that is *the* grace of the contemplative: he or she knows *when* and *how* to be ministered to. Such persons have learned how to receive, how to be open, how to be touched. They are not resistant to grace and therefore can be both patient and hopeful. Contemplatives know how to wait and joyfully anticipate the inbreak of God. They have learned how to obey the divine command, "Be still, and know that I am God" (Psalm 46:10). And this one: "Wait on the Lord: be of good courage, and he shall strengthen thine heart: wait, I say, on the Lord" (Psalm 27:14, AV). But contemplatives should not set this in opposition to Paul's admonition that when one gives aid it should be done zealously; in fact he too gave a command: "Never flag in zeal" (Romans 12:8,11).

Holy Scripture is perfectly comfortable in putting zeal and waiting together. They are not antithetical to each other and one is not superior to the other. They stand in a necessary tension with each other. Zeal keeps waiting from being pure inactivity. Waiting keeps zeal from being fanaticism. And when it comes to practice, the person who is perpetually active and always available is not fit to be available. Likewise the contemplative needs to be careful lest he or she be impressed with his or her own religiousness. Attentiveness to Christ is not shown just by a personal life of prayer and meditation. There is also the Christ to be attended to who is in "the least of these"—the imprisoned, the hungry, the naked, the thirsty, and the stranger (Matthew 25:31ff.).

The life of Jesus certainly shows that he both prayed and served. But I do not think that he ever said or did anything that would indicate that if he had his druthers, as we say, he would rank retreat and prayer over service. The point has already been argued that Jesus prayed what he confessed, he confessed what he prayed, and lived out both what he prayed and confessed. This is clearly seen in the incidental and intentional aspects of his life and work.

With regard to the *incidental* aspect, one might cite a passage such as the visit with the Samaritan woman (John 4). It was unplanned and it was unconventional. But neither the *abruptness* of its occurrence nor the *awkwardness* of the situation (the woman had scandal written all over her life) deterred Jesus. Both *abruptness* and *awkwardness* are frequent accompaniments of a sensitive life. The good Samaritan was well aware of that (Luke 10:25ff.). Both he and Jesus had experiential understanding of a line in Archibald MacLeish's poem, *J.B.:* "Chosen by the act of having seen." The vocation is made obvious in the event. You do not choose the event. The event chooses you. The summons to act is its own form of consecration, unwanted and unwelcome as it might be. As Paul Scherer said in one of his sermons, "Life never says please." That which appears to be incidental turns out to be integral to the spiritual life.

The *intentional* aspect of Jesus' life and work has been made significant to me in the meal stories (Proverbs 9:1-6; Matthew 8:9-13; Luke 14:12-14; 7:36-50). The meals with publicans and sinners in particular manifested a profound sense of Christ's vocation in giving place to those who had none. What better way was there to do it than at table? The focus is on Jesus' intention to create community with and for publicans and sinners. The courage required for something as unconventional as that allowed a certain sense of personal authority to assert itself. What Jesus did he did in and through his body, knowing full well the costs that it entailed. At table, he made himself present *to* and *for* his guests.

Lutheran theology, as we have noted, speaks of God's *promeity,* i.e. the "for me-ness" of God in Christ. Such is also present in the words of Luther's friend, Philipp Melanchthon: "To know Christ is to know his benefits." The major benefit to be known through Christ is that God is "for me." Christ Jesus intentionally communicated this bodily, as he made himself present to the woman taken in adultery, in the calling of Matthew the tax collector, in touching lepers, in giving place in the kingdom to the thief on the cross, and in ministering to the likes of the woman from Tyre and Sidon. In short, his intentional acts were both the sign and the conveyance of the kingdom.

These biblical factors are bound to have an effect on spiritual theology. If, for example, one would read in tandem E.B. Workman's classic, *The Evolution of the Monastic Ideal,*[2] and Johannes Metz's *Theology of the World,*[3] one would immediately see a difference. Workman argued that monasticism and the ascetic ideal were exercises in renunciation of the world. Metz, on the other hand, argues that asceticism is really an exercise in affirmation of the world, as, it might be added, Carl Braaten has argued in this country.[4]

Metz portrays the crucifixion as the deepest demonstration of love for the world and affirmation of the world's right to be. The death of Christ for the world is the affirmation of creation. He describes the crucifixion as the primary model for Christian existence. He also argues that such love as the crucifixion demonstrates is a rehearsal of hope against hope. The crucified one laid down his life for the world, in solidarity with the world. It is a statement of God's commitment *to* and steadfast love *for* what he had made. It is we who are to show God's continuing love for what he has made by bearing our crosses and thus "filling up what is lacking in the sufferings of Christ. . . " (Colossians 1:24).

If one returns to the liturgical theme introduced in a previous chapter, one finds a similar line of discussion as that found in Metz and Braaten. From Alexander Schmemann as a representative of Eastern Orthodoxy to the Lutheran Frank Senn, one finds a discussion of the eventual monastic distortion of prayer.[5] Both argue that monasticism lost its tension with the world and withdrew into its own community. Why? Monasticism surrendered a sense of the between, of space between itself and the world. It had no time for the world. Thus it lost a life of prayer in relation to the world. Since the world was to be denied and the flesh was a prison, prayer increasingly became a discipline unto itself, thus manifesting a form of denial of the world. In no way was prayer a mode of being in the world and a mode of being for the world. Prayer was its own vocation, instead of prayer being a way of perfecting the person in the world and maybe even a way of perfecting the world through the person. The monastic person sought only the perfection of prayer. When that takes place, spirituality has become spiritualism and has set up the conditions for its own demise. Theologically, such a condition is what the Augustinian-Lutheran tradition has said is the basic nature of sin: a person or situation curved in upon itself. More graphically portrayed, there is a simile used by a Russian spiritual father, Theophan the Recluse, to the effect that such a self-centeredness is like the thin shaving that flies off when a carpenter planes a board: all it does is circle about itself.

Prophetic or servant spirituality is beginning to form its own method and literature, a development described by John Coburn and Urban Holmes[6] as the decline of spirituality by the manual and/or prayer book method. What is on the rise is best illustrated by Michel Quoist's book, *Prayers.*[7] The method of this spirituality is structured into the form of praying.

Quoist includes three things in prayer-form: 1) a life-situation arising out of his work as a priest-social worker among the disenfranchized, the unwanted, or the forgotten people; 2) a Scripture passage that parallels the situation; and 3) a narrative prayer that he uses to process the situation and to reflect on his own attempt to relate to it truthfully—while at at the same time perceiving Christ's relation to it. As he perceives Christ's relation to it, so he perceives his own. Thus he structures his own life as a "little Christ." Here is a sample:

> . . . *I know that in one single room thirteen crowded people are breathing on one another.*
>
> *I know a mother who hooks the table and the chairs to the ceiling to make room for mattresses.*
>
> *I know that rats come out to eat the crusts, and bite the babies.*
>
> *I know a father who gets up to stretch oilcloth above the rain-soaked bed of his four children.*
>
> *I know a mother who stays up all night, since there is room for only one bed, and the two children are sick.*
>
> *I know a drunken father who vomits on the child sleeping beside him.*
>
> *I know a big boy who runs away alone into the night because he can't take it any more. . . .*
>
> *I know a wife who avoids her husband, as there is no room for another baby at home.*
>
> *I know a child who is quietly dying, soon to join his four little brothers.*
>
> *I know. . . .*
>
> *I know hundreds of others—yet I was going to sleep peacefully between my nice white sheets.*
>
> *I wish I didn't know, Lord.*
>
> *I wish it were not true.*
>
> *I wish I could convince myself that I'm dreaming.*
>
> *I wish someone could prove that I'm exaggerating.*
>
> *I wish they'd show me that all these people have only themselves to blame, that it's all their fault they are so miserable.*
>
> *I'd like to be reassured, Lord, but I can't be.*
>
> *It's too late.*
>
> *I've seen too much.*
>
> *I've counted too much, and, Lord, these ruthless figures have robbed me forever of my innocent tranquility.*

These prayers are filled with the lament of the have-nots, of those shut-out, unwanted, those who are so bitter that they do not *want* to be wanted, the sexually abused and abusing—you name it and you'll find it in Quoist. What Quoist has done, both as a priest-social worker and as a practitioner of the prayed life, is to have drawn near, as Jesus did, to those who belong to no one and nowhere. What Quoist will do by his companionship and compassion is to affirm and embody God's steadfast love for them. Note the word "compassion," which means a shared suffering. He shared the suffering of the poor and the suffering of Christ *for* the poor. This is part of filling up what is lacking in the sufferings of Christ. It goes on wherever God's creatures belong to no one and nowhere. This is what Metz meant by self-denial as world affirmation. We do not depreciate self and world. Anything that depreciates seems to be of less and less value. Rather, we are to value what Jesus valued—the poor, the homeless, the unwanted. His sacrifice for them made their value an ultimate worth. Thus in affirming what Jesus valued, we deny only that personal value which interferes with our loving what Jesus loved.

Read the meditations of the French priest Jean Vanier in his *Be Not Afraid,*[8] or those of Mother Teresa of Calcutta.[9] The genre is the same as that of Quoist. Or take Philip Berrigan's *Uncommon Prayers,*[10] the prayed reflections of one who has drawn near to some American dilemmas, or the smuggled-out publication of Father Dmitrii Dudko's Moscow dialogue sermons, *Our Hope,*[11] so hot that Dudko is unwanted in Moscow.

There is an increasingly remarkable spiritual literature to be found of the "letters from prison" type:

Dietrich Bonhoeffer, *Letters and Papers from Prison,* new, enlarged edition, ed. Eberhard Bethge and tr. Reginald Fuller, et al. (New York: The Macmillan Company, 1972).

Alfred Delp, S.J. *The Prison Meditations of Father Delp,* intro. by Thomas Merton (New York: The Macmillan Company, 1963).

Helmut Gollwitzer, Kathe Kuhn, Reinhold Schneider, eds., tr. Reinhard Kuhn, *Dying We Live* (New York: The Seabury Press, 1968).

Carlos Alberto Libiano Christo, *Against Principalities and Powers. Letters from a Brazilian Jail,* trans. John Drury (Maryknoll: Orbis Books, 1971).

In all this let not the earlier distinction I made in the life of Jesus be overlooked: there are *incidental* aspects to spirituality, unplanned and unanticipated. But the *intentional* aspect is what begs for attention now. It is through the intentional life that the unique character of Christianity is revealed—as the Cronin story, mentioned previously, shows. Grace takes the initiative to create a "between" where there is none. It's that simple.

But at that very point I make a personal distinction. In the common parlance of Christians there is much talk about bearing burdens and carrying crosses. The distinction between them is crucial. People refer to illnesses, financial reverses, and personal tensions as crosses. I do not think they are and I say this as one who has endured a catastrophic illness, although I readily admit to some oversimplification here. If every burden is a cross, then the word is emptied of its meaning. Illnesses are burdens and have no volitional aspect. To be sure, there is a volitional aspect involved in having to deal with them truthfully, in "owning" them as our own. But to take up a cross is an *intentional* act. A cross, in my opinion, is to initiate a ministry or relationship knowing full well that it may be rejected by those being served and/or repudiated by family, friends, or neighbors. A cross-bearer knows that and thus is aware that in addition to initiative there must be integrity. What is begun must be carried through, as the Cronin story again illustrates. Cross-bearers suffer, the just for the unjust. What is initiated must have a maintenance factor. What fastens the cross-bearer to the cross, said Salvador Dali, is love, not nails. Hence one of his paintings, grotesque though it is, is of a space between Jesus and the cross behind him, with the nails showing and Jesus suspended in mid-air. When asked why he painted such a picture, Dali is supposed to have answered, "Something other than the nails held him there." Those on whom we *set* our affection we *serve* with affection. Those who resent our service, ridicule our interest in the poor, the lost, and the overlooked need compassion, not censure. A cross is a ministry or relationship initiated in compassion, not condescension, knowing full well that cross-bearers are seldom admired and regularly resented. But I know of few ministries without the cross since the chief Minister, the Lord and Bishop of our souls, even Jesus Christ, had a cross for his altar and the sacrifice on it was himself.

Let us pray that in being alive in Christ we will become more alert to life. Let us also pray that in being alert to the world we will be more alive to Christ, who is at work in the world for the sake of the world.

# ENDNOTES

1. Introduction by Frederick Tolles, John Greenleaf Whittier Edition (New York: Corinth Books, 1961).
2. Foreword by David Knowles (Boston: Beacon Press, 1962).
3. *Theology of the World,* tr. William Glen-Doppel (New York: The Seabury Press, 1973).
4. *Christ and Counter Christ* (Philadelphia: Fortress Press, 1972).
5. Senn, *The Pastor As Worship Leader* (Minneapolis: Augsburg Publishing House, 1977), chapter 2.
6. John Coburn, "The New Mood in Spirituality," in *Spirituality for Today,* ed. Eric James (London: SCM Press, Ltd., 1968), and Urban Holmes, "A Taxonomy of Contemporary Spirituality" in *Christians at Prayer,* ed. John Gallen, S.J. (Notre Dame and London: University of Notre Dame Press, 1977).
7. Translated by Agnes M. Forsyth and Anne Marie de Commaille (New York: Avon Books, 1975). Quoted with permission of Sheed and Ward.
8. (New York, et al.: Paulist Press, 1975).
9. Mother Teresa, *A Gift for God: Prayers and Meditations,* introduction by Malcolm Muggeridge (San Francisco, et al.: Harper and Row, 1975); *Life in the Spirit: Reflections, Meditations, and Prayers,* ed. Kathryn Spink (San Francisco, et al.: Harper and Row, 1983).
10. Illustrations by Robert McGovern (New York: The Seabury Press, 1978).
11. Translated by Paul D. Garrett and Foreword by John Meyendorf (Crestwood: St. Vladimir's Press, 1977).